Managing For Service Quality

by

Chris Skelcher

LONGMAN

Published by Longman Industry and Public Service
Management, Longman Group UK Ltd, 6th Floor, Westgate
House, The High, Harlow, Essex CM20 1YR
Telephone: Harlow (0279) 442601; Fax: Harlow (0279) 444501;
Telex: 81491 Padlog

A catalogue record for this book is available from the British Library

ISBN 0-582-09587-5

Printed in Malaysia by TCP

Contents

The Local Government Management Board is governed by a board of elected members nominated by the local authority associations. It represents the interests of local authorities throughout the country. At present there are separate financial arrangements covering the provision of services, including publications, to Scottish authorities.

By focusing on management and human resource issues, LGMB helps local authorities to be more effective in their work, the way they deliver services and the way they provide democratic leadership in their communities. It seeks contributions and suggestions from local authorities to enable it to provide a responsive, relevant service.

Preface

This book covers a wide range of issues which are presented in a number of different ways. At some points it is specific and highly practical while elsewhere the discussion is more conceptual. Partly this is deliberate – it is important to have the wider overview and perspective as well as the detailed implications – but it is also inevitable when local authorities are only now attempting to put particular ideas into practice. Total quality management and empowerment are two examples. In both cases the theory is available but the practice is limited. Hopefully our learning over the next few years will be rapid and the gaps in this book filled!

In writing this book I have drawn on the encouragement and ideas offered by many people, unfortunately too numerous to mention individually. However my particular thanks go to Kieron Walsh, John Stewart and Michael Clarke for speedily and helpfully commenting on the draft of the book, to Barbara Webster for her consistent support and clear thinking and to Chris Game for his experience of market research on which I have drawn in Chapter 3. To my children Tom and Lizzie I owe a special 'thank you' for putting up with my occasional distractions over the past few months.

Chris Skelcher
January 1992

1 The service revolution

The service revolution which has swept the commercial sector in the last decade has also found its way into the public service, producing changes which are transforming thinking about the relationships between local authorities and their communities. Indeed the use of the term *customer* or *consumer* to refer to those previously described as *clients, tenants, residents* and *claimants* is a visible indication of the profound and deep-seated changes which are now occurring. It signifies a questioning and rejection of the traditional model of uniform services being delivered to passive recipients who had little voice or influence, and its replacement by a view that those receiving services should have choice and be actively involved in the process of deciding what is to be provided, when, how and by whom.

Across the public sector there has been a strong momentum to put customers first:

- Inland Revenue has developed a taxpayer's charter defining the rights of customers.
- Health authorities have appointed quality assurance managers to improve service delivery in hospitals.
- British Rail provides financial compensation to customers whose train is significantly delayed.
- Magistrates' courts are required to conduct customer surveys, and the findings are incorporated into the national management information system.
- The National Audit Office has undertaken a study of social security customers' experiences which is being used by the new Social Security Agency to improve service quality.

Local authorities, because of their range of functions, active local political dimension and direct impact on customers and citizens have been in the forefront of initiatives to develop a customer orientation and improve service quality. Variously termed the *public service orientation, customer care* or *putting people first*, these initiatives have included customer surveys, improvements in reception areas, consultation with service users, redesign of service systems and the specification of customers' rights.

Improving service quality in local government

Citizens' and customers' concern about the quality of local government and its services is not new. During the 1960s and 1970s planning, housing and highways projects frequently met with opposition from affected groups. The communities involved, while wanting improvements in housing conditions and transport systems, did not always regard the schemes proposed by local authorities as the most appropriate and sometimes felt that they had been excluded from the decisions being made about their future. The Skeffington Report and subsequent development of public participation in planning and urban renewal were attempts to improve the relationship between the local authority and the public as well as the quality of the decision process and the decisions themselves.

During the 1970s several local authorities developed area management schemes designed to enhance public involvement and improve service delivery. These initiatives took various forms but common to all was the desire to match services more effectively to the needs of particular localities. In some cases the project involved little more than the identification of the needs of different areas within the authority using a range of social indicators. Elsewhere area teams or even member committees were established, occasionally becoming an integral part of the authority's political, managerial and financial processes. Tenant participation in housing became more extensive and local authorities began to appoint community development officers to assist groups with a common interest to organise and articulate their views to the council. There were also some experiments with employee participation and industrial democracy in local government.

In the last decade there have been three major developments. Firstly a number of local authorities have recognised that their communities are not uniform and that some groups are differentially disadvantaged in society as a whole and in terms of local public services. Consequently a series of equal opportunity initiatives have been undertaken including the creation of specialist units and committees and the development of liaison and consultation arrangements with black and ethnic minority communities, women, pensioners and disabled people and other groups. In addition greater support has been given to the voluntary sector to assist them to meet particular needs.

Secondly there has been a new wave of management thinking stimulated by the service movement in the private sector and codified in books by Peters and Waterman (1982) and Normann (1984). Peters' and Waterman's *In Search of Excellence* has been particularly influential in highlighting eight factors which they believe contribute to organisational success:

- A bias for action – solving problems when and where they arise, and acting quickly rather than taking a long time to analyse the problem and respond.
- Close to the customer – listening to and learning from customers and taking steps to use that information to improve quality.
- Autonomy and entrepreneurship – giving employees the discretion and authority to make decisions and try out new ideas.
- Productivity through people – investing in employees and fostering their commitment to the quality of the organisation's services.

- Hands-on, value driven – managers regularly visiting and being involved in the work of their sections, and through their behaviour conveying the organisation's core values.
- Stick to the knitting – concentrate on those activities which are the organisation's core business and do those well.
- Simple form, lean staff – keeping a simple and clear organisational structure with a small corporate centre.
- Simultaneous loose-tight properties – highly decentralised organisations which have considerable discretion around a core of corporate values.

These ideas have had a significant influence on management practice in local authorities. So too have the writings of John Stewart and Michael Clarke (1987) who have sought to articulate a new sense of purpose for local government by focussing on the public service orientation which they define as:

- a local authority's activities exist to provide service for the public;
- a local authority will be judged by the quality of service provided within the resources available;
- the service provided is only of real value if it is of value to those for whom it is provided;
- those for whom services are provided are customers demanding high quality service;
- quality of service demands closeness to the customer.

Subsequent work by the Local Government Management Board (1987; 1989) developed this theme and its practical implications for local authorities.

Finally the legislative and resource context imposed by central government and the political values of elected councillors have combined to produce a greater concern to build improved relationships with customers and develop service quality. Compulsory competitive tendering (CCT), local management of schools (LMS), opting out in education, housing action trusts (HATs), the role of the Audit Commission, community charge, community care legislation and other factors have created a climate in which longstanding quality issues could be addressed and action swiftly taken.

In the 1990s there has been a consolidation of these earlier themes, especially in the proposals of the major political parties for improving public services. From its policy review following the 1987 general election the Labour Party published *Quality Street* – a programme to improve the quality of local government services and build a partnership between the council and the community. *Quality Street* proposed a number of specific measures, including:

- service guarantees for each activity, including redress mechanisms and financial compensation where a fee is charged;
- minimum standards of employee training;
- introducing a power of general competence;
- increasing citizen and customer control of services;

- quality audits of local authority services to assess value for people and value for money;
- alternatives to compulsory competitive tendering;
- employee participation;
- a quality commission to promote the quality of local government services.

A number of these ideas have been piloted in Labour local authorities and the lessons learnt have contributed to the Labour Party's *Citizen's Charter* which was published in 1991. This document elaborates the themes contained in *Quality Street* as well as covering other issues not directly related to local government.

A key policy initiative in John Major's first year of office as Prime Minister has been the Conservative government's *Citizen's Charter* (Prime Minister 1991). This was launched in the summer of 1991 with the aim of making 'public services answer better to the wishes of their users and to raise their overall quality'. The *Charter* proposes seven principles of public service:

- Standards – explicit statements covering employee behaviour and levels of service which should be prominently displayed.
- Openness – about how public services are run, how much they cost and whether they are meeting their standards.
- Information – full and accurate information in plain language.
- Choice – public consultation and choice offered wherever possible.
- Non-discrimination – services should be available regardless of race or sex.
- Accessibility – services should be run to suit the convenience of customers.
- Redress – a well-publicised and readily available complaints procedure.

The Government proposes to introduce a Chartermark for those services which can be independently validated as meeting the *Charter* standards. Like the Labour Party document this *Citizen's Charter* covers a range of public services. Its proposals to raise the quality of local government services include:

- an improved Tenants' Charter;
- lay assessors on schools tribunals dealing with admissions, exclusions or statementing and a range of other education proposals subsequently elaborated in the *Parents' Charter* (DES 1991);
- extending compulsory competitive tendering;
- Audit Commission to publish league tables of local authority performance;
- targets for police response times;
- local lay adjudicators to deal with minor claims for redress;
- local authorities required to publish their response to the auditor's report.

The Liberal Democrats have also recently produced a policy paper on local government (Liberal Democrats 1991). This has a particularly strong emphasis on citizens and citizenship in its proposals for the devolution of power to local communities, reform of the electoral system and increased local self-determination. Local authorities would also be required to publish a *Charter of Services* defining basic levels which individuals were entitled to receive and a system of internal and external ombudspeople would be available to deal with complaints and redress.

The quality of local authority and other public services has therefore emerged as a key element in the competition between the major political parties and is likely to lead to further legislative change. In the proposals of all three main political parties there is a desire to ensure that service standards are specified and clear redress mechanisms exist.

Managing for service quality

Building service quality in a local authority is a key management task for the 1990s. This book covers the main issues managers, elected members and others working in or concerned about the quality of services need to understand and provides a series of practical examples.

Customers and the local authority (Chapter 2) discusses who local authority customers are and highlights in particular the difference between the customers of a commercial concern and those of a local authority. It explores the way in which customers evaluate service quality and specifies the criteria local authorities should take into account in designing services from a customer perspective. The extent to which local authorities meet these criteria is examined and blockages to better service identified. Finally different approaches to service quality are discussed.

Reviewing services (Chapter 3) explores a series of approaches to assessing and evaluating existing provision and identifying new requirements. It covers the overall design of the review process, direct and indirect methods of research and consultation. The chapter concludes by discussing quality audits.

Key elements in service review and design (Chapter 4) outlines concepts which are central to developing quality and discusses their practical application. Issues covered include need and demand, equality and discrimination, economy, efficiency and effectiveness and rationing. The chapter also presents a series of criteria against which different patterns of service organisation and delivery can be assessed.

Designing the service relationship (Chapter 5) highlights the detailed practical steps to improving the quality of local authority services. It includes sections on specifying the service package, designing the customer process, the role of customer-contact employees, service guarantees and complaints systems.

Councillors and citizens – the political dimension (Chapter 6) takes a wider view and addresses the overall relationship between the local authority and its citizens. Starting with a discussion of the councillor's role in service quality the chapter goes on to explore active citizenship and empowerment.

Approaches to empowerment and the involvement of customers and citizens are highlighted.

Organising for service quality (Chapter 7) reviews the various ways in which local authorities can organise themselves and assesses these in terms of their impact on service quality. After discussing the strengths and weaknesses of the conventional service department/committee arrangement the chapter covers strategic management, decentralisation, devolved management and the client/contractor or purchaser/provider model. Approaches to working with the voluntary sector are also discussed in detail.

Service quality – the management agenda (Chapter 8) focuses on managers themselves and the internal organisational issues to which they must respond. After discussing quality systems, front-line/back-line relationships and employee development the manager's role in building service quality is explored. This is followed by a discussion of the way in which a service culture can be developed.

Strategies for service quality (Chapter 9) explores the implementation of the initiatives discussed earlier in the book. It highlights the nature of and process for developing strategy and the particular components which should be included in any strategy for service quality. Finally ways of managing the organisational change involved are reviewed.

2 Customers and the local authority

Looks of puzzlement and bemusement would greet the person who, as recently as the mid 1980s, referred to the *customers* of the local authority. In recent years the term has come into widespread use and is commonly taken to refer to anyone who receives a local authority service, however indirect that relationship may be.

This chapter starts by exploring the ways in which the concept of a customer has been rooted in private sector thinking and highlights the limitations of this model for the public sector. The idea of a local authority customer – some prefer the term consumer (see below) – is then set in context by discussing the types of relationships between members of the community and local government. Internal customers within other parts of the local authority are also discussed. The chapter continues by exploring the ways in which customers evaluate service quality and the constraints which it is necessary for the local authority to overcome if it is to develop a customer orientation. Finally a framework for mapping different local authority approaches to service quality is presented.

Customers in the private sector

As a result of the Excellence movement and the pressure to establish quasi-commercial relationships in the public sector (Chapter 1) the idea of the customer has developed a strong ideological connotation. It has become associated with the service relationships presented in TV advertisements for banks, airlines, car hire firms and fast-food restaurants – individuals having the resources to choose a product which is delivered in a high-quality environment by helpful and thoughtful staff. The interaction is presented as unproblematic and all participants leave satisfied – the customer with what they wanted and staff with a sense of having completed a transaction and provided good service. Here, for example, is the view of a leading writer on service quality: 'In a well designed service delivery system we will find that the employee (and) the client . . . all emerge with an enhanced sense of self-esteem.' (Normann 1984, p.18) This has become a model for the local authority to aspire to, but is this really what it is like for all or indeed most private sector customers? And is it appropriate for a public service organisation?

The power of customers in the market sector is said to rest on their ability to purchase a product from one supplier rather than another. In order to stay in business, firms must satisfy customer demands for particular products and for the service relationships through which they are provided (for example the appearance of employees, promptness of delivery and so on, see below). In practice however the power of private sector customers is not always so clear cut. Firstly they may lack sufficient financial resources to enable them to exercise effective choice – or even to have basic needs met. For those on low incomes market choice is a luxury seldom experienced in any real sense, as the young people in London's cardboard city or families existing in low-grade rented accommodation would testify. Secondly everyday experience and the evidence of watchdogs such as the Consumers' Association and trading standards departments demonstrates that customers can (sometimes knowingly) be sold faulty or incorrectly described products and subsequently have considerable difficulty in implementing their statutory rights and obtaining redress. The package holiday industry in the 1970s provides a graphic example of this problem. Finally marketing and advertising are used to stimulate new demands and widespread access to credit turns potential customers into actual ones. A central part of many private sector business plans, for example, is to increase market share by encouraging someone else's customers to switch loyalties as well as creating new purchasers.

The customer orientation in the market sector is therefore by no means as unproblematic as it is often presented. In developing a focus on customers local authorities should be aware of the values and tensions which underlie its use in the commercial sector and root their initiatives firmly in a public service ethos.

The local authority customer

Because of the nature of the public service the imitation of a private sector customer focus is not wholly appropriate. For example, the recipients of many public services 'are not in any meaningful sense "consumers" . . . because they do not have an alternative outlet to "shop" at.' (Fry 1987, p.436) Those receiving education, social services, domestic refuse collection, low-income housing and leisure facilities face a monopoly or near-monopoly provider – the local authority. The picture is compounded further by the varied nature of services provided:

- access to some activities is rationed and not all wanting the service will obtain it, for example local authority housing and literacy classes;
- in other services it is impossible to restrict an individual's use of or benefits from the service, for example street lighting and emergency planning;
- car parking controls and trading standards are amongst the regulatory services, benefitting one group (shoppers in the latter case) but being seen by others (traders selling misdescribed goods) as undesirable;

- some are enabling, for example libraries and the provision of play areas;
- some are free at the point of delivery, for example primary education and footpath maintenance;
- some charge, for example meals on wheels and planning applications.

Additionally, and unlike the market sector, customers are *citizens* able to influence the policy of the provider through the local political system. With certain limited exceptions there is universal franchise for all over the age of eighteen years. Members of the community can vote for particular candidates in local elections or indeed stand for election themselves. Further, and unlike the directors of many private sector companies, local councillors are accessible and visible figures in their communities. Their names and private addresses are in the public domain, they represent a specific local constituency and are available to act as problem-solvers and advocates in customers' dealings with the local authority to which they have been elected. There is also a high degree of openness in local authority decision-making compared with either the private sector or other public sector agencies. The Local Government (Access to Information) Act together with other service-specific legislation establishes procedures for public access to decision-making forums and files as well as the right to be consulted on particular classes of decision (for example planning developments). Complaints and appeals procedures are also a statutory requirement in several areas of service. This relationship between the citizen and the local authority is discused in greater detail in Chapter 6.

Because of the nature of local government and local authority services the term customer can refer to:

- the direct user of the service;
- the direct or indirect recipient of a local authority's activity;
- those gaining benefit or disbenefit from local authority activity or inactivity; and
- stakeholders who do not fall into any of the above groups but nevertheless have an interest in the service (for example as a taxpayer).

This is illustrated in Figure 2.1 with reference to enabling and regulatory local government services.

While many local authorities now use the term customer some believe that it conveys an image of commercial, market relationships which is inappropriate to the public service. *Consumer* is frequently used as an alternative. This too has its difficulties, particularly when applied to regulatory services – where customer also seems inappropriate. Using customer or consumer to describe a restaurant owner being prosecuted under the environmental health legislation or a caravan dweller being evicted from council-owned waste land stretches the imagination! There is no ideal generic term to describe those who receive – in whatever way – the benefits or disbenefits of local authority activity. In this book the term customer is used, but the examples throughout the chapters serve to highlight that it

Figure 2.1: Meanings of customer

Type of Service	Enabling Service (e.g. under 5s provision)	Regulatory Service (e.g. trading standards)
User	Children under 5 years at local authority supported facility	Person making a complaint to local authority about a faulty good
Recipient	As above	The trader who sold the faulty good
Beneficiary	The child, the child's parents, the mother's employer, prospective employers gaining advantage from early education of children	The complainant, other customers at that shop, the shop (if concerned about its reputation)
Stakeholder	Women who may have children in the future, groups concerned about children's welfare	Manufacturers, groups concerned with shoppers' rights

refers to the range of local government services, not just those where a commercial or quasi-market relationship occurs.

The internal customer

So far attention has been focussed on external customers of local government services, but increasingly local authorities are organised in terms of internal clients or purchasers and contractors or providers. The advent of compulsory competitive tendering, local management of schools, the community care legislation, devolved management and service level agreements (SLAs) have hightened and clarified the relationships within local authorities. Client departments are clearly identified as customers of the direct service organisation (DSO), front-line services are recognised as the customer for personnel and other central services and resource centre managers the customer for finance services. Just as with the external customer, so questions of service quality are important. Should the residential home manager, for example, be required to purchase payroll services from the finance department; or is there freedom to gather competitive quotes from a variety of commercial concerns and contract with an outside business if it is cheaper? These issues are discussed in greater detail in Chapter 7.

There are therefore strong parallels between the position of internal and external customers in their relationship to those with the power to determine the type and nature of services to be provided. While the rest of this chapter focusses on external customers many of the points explored are also directly transferable to internal customers.

Customers and service quality

Adopting the customer as the focus for improvements in service quality requires local authorities to change their thinking in three main ways (Figure 2.2).

- It places attention on the specific individual and their particular needs and requirements rather than seeing that person just as part of a larger group. It is about personalising or customising the *service package* – the bundle of activities, interactions and resources that form the relationship between the customer and the agency. The service should be delivered to meet the customer's needs not the predispositions, assumptions and rationale of the agency.
- There are implications for the power relationship between customer and producer since consumerism challenges a long-standing practice of the Welfare State that those who used its services should be passive recipients minimally involved in policy-making and service design and having limited choice. Instead the local authority should seek to maximise people's involvement in shaping and determining the choices available to them.
- The traditional assumptions informing the local authority service delivery function are challenged. Rather than paternalism, barriers to access and a dominance of organisational definitions the concern is with service quality – overcoming the locational, informational, personal and other constraints which hinder the relationship between customer and local authority and ensuring that customer's needs are met.

Figure 2.2: The public and a customer: points of comparison

	The Public	**A Customer**
Identity	Generalised group	Specific individual
Degree of power	Limited	Extensive
Service assumptions	Paternalism	Quality

How customers evaluate service quality

Delivering quality service requires an understanding of the way customers evaluate the service package and the ability to identify the quality gap between expected and perceived service. While this may be relatively straightforward for road repairs and refuse collection in other activities it is more complex. A number of services are only created in the interaction between customer and employee. For example local authorities have the potential to provide a high quality educational experience. While its ability to realise this will be affected by class size, school resources and the home environment, a crucial factor is the skill of the teacher in interaction with individual pupils. This also applies in the home help field where the ability to gain and maintain the confidence and trust of older people is a vital yet unquantifiable component of service quality. Consequently the past experiences, existing predispositions and emotional states of both customers and employees can result in differing interpretations of a service encounter. Such subjectivity also leads to different levels of expectation amongst customers – for 90 per cent of customers to say that high quality service was provided may look good at first sight, but if they had very low expectations in the first place this is no cause for satisfaction!

In the private sector, considerable research has been undertaken into the way in which customers evaluate service quality. A distinction is commonly drawn between:

- The core service – referring to the specific goods or services required. For example in buying a washing machine the customer might evaluate quality in terms of the machine's specified performance, its appearance, the guarantee offered and ease of access to after-sales service; the council tenant might evaluate quality in relation to speed of the repairs service, frequency and standard of grounds maintenance and (in high-rise blocks) ability to use the waste chute without it becoming blocked.
- The peripherals – which are not an essential part of the product or the customer's requirements but nevertheless are of benefit. For example a free packet of washing powder, a demonstration of the machine in the customer's own home, a free service call after three months and coffee and biscuits when viewing the machine at the show-room; or for the council tenant a comfortable waiting area at the housing office or regular information on new initiatives which affect the estate.

As a result of service quality improvements and changing social attitudes so customers begin to expect what were formerly peripherals to be part of the core service.

Stewart and Walsh (1989) use these ideas to develop a three-fold framework for evaluating service quality:

- the core service, that is whether the service does what it is designed to do;
- the service surroundings, that is the physical conditions within which the service is provided:
- the service relationships, that is the relationship between those providing and those receiving the service.

They argue that these are interlinked and part of the customer's total experience of the service and therefore provide the basis for the evaluation of quality. The priority accorded to each, however, will vary from service to service. In using a park, for example, the service surroundings are likely to be of more weight than the service relationship.

When taking concepts and frameworks from the private sector, however, it is important to ensure that they meet the special conditions of local government. In this respect the quality framework developed by Stewart and Walsh fails to take account of the one ingredient stressed in the consumerist literature – power. For example the power to choose, taken for granted in private sector models, is conspicuously absent from many aspects of the customer's interactions with local authorities. Other facets of customer power could include the power to influence and the power to obtain redress. Their framework is primarily about the service assumptions held by the local authority rather than the degree of power accorded to the customer (see Figure 2.2). Yet power is also a criteria for judging service quality and a particularly important one for customers of the public sector (Figure 2.3).

Figure 2.3: The four elements of service quality

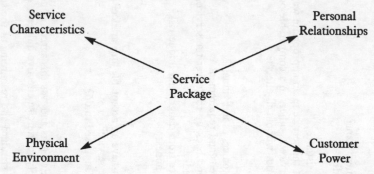

These four dimensions of service quality are specified in more detail in Figure 2.4. Not all components will be relevant or appropriate to every service, but they provide a basis from which local authorities can begin to develop a customer evaluation of their services.

The service package

Undertaking an evaluation of service quality involves reviewing the service package provided by the local authority from the customer's perspective. The service package – the mix of activities, resources and policies – is defined in terms of most if not all the elements listed in Figure 2.4. However it is likely that there will be differences between:

- the service package that is desired or sought by actual or potential customers;
- the service package that members and officers have designed; and
- the service package the authority is delivering through the actual operation of policies and procedures and the actions of employees at different levels in the organisation.

For example:

As a result of market research and consultation with users and community groups a district council leisure committee agreed a set of women-only activities, including regular evening swimming sessions. Because the

Figure 2.4: Customer criteria for evaluating service quality in local government

Service characteristics

AVAILABILITY	Does the agency provide the service customers want?
STANDARDS	Is the service available at the right standard?
TIMELINESS	Is the service available at a good time?
RELIABILITY	Is the service accurate, dependable and consistent?
INFORMATION	Does the agency provide information about the service in an appropriate way?
EQUALITY	Will customers receive the same level of service as others in a comparable or similar position?
PERFORMANCE	Does the service do what it is supposed to do, without ill effects?

The personal relationship

COURTESY	Are employees polite and do they treat customers as individuals?
RESPONSIVENESS	Are employees responsive to customers' needs and requirements?
COMPETENCE	Do employees have the skills, knowledge and back-up to deliver the service?
COMMUNICATION	Are customers listened to and kept informed?
SECURITY	Do employees ensure that customers are free from danger and undue risk?
CREDIBILITY	Are employers trustworthy, believable and honest?

The service setting

APPEARANCE	Do the building, employees and equipment have an acceptable appearance?
ACCESS	Can customers physically gain access to the service?
FUNCTIONING	Does the physical equipment do what it is supposed to do?

The customer's power

RIGHTS	Do customers have a clear statement of their rights and was this agreed in consultation with them?
VOICE	Do customers have the right and opportunity to exercise effective influence on services and the overall policy framework?
CHOICE	Do customers have choice over the nature, standard and resourcing of the service?
REDRESS	Is there a clear means of making representations to the local authority where service is not appropriate or fails to meet standards, and of obtaining suitable redress?

swimming pool is located in a park and many potential women users did not have access to a car their concern about safety meant that usage was low in the winter months. As a result the pool supervisor, who was also under pressure to maximise income, decided to permit a water-polo team to hire half the pool for their practice sessions. This resulted in a further decrease in usage by women swimmers and ultimately the facility was withdrawn because of a perceived lack of demand by customers.

In this example the service package desired by women in the community was only partly provided. Women-only sessions were programmed but the service package which was designed failed to take any account of the environment of the pool and the question of personal safety. Members and senior managers also assumed that the designed service package was being provided, but the pool staff delivered an adapted package (retaining space for women but allowing other users in part of the pool). This resulted in a greater gap between the women customers' expectations and the reality, hence reducing usage. It is therefore important for local authorities to be clear *which* service package they are evaluating and to be able to identify any discrepancy between desired, designed and delivered service packages.

The existence of differing service package definitions has been revealed from research into private sector service industries as well as UK local authorities. One study of service industries, in which focussed discussions were held with customers and providers, revealed five major quality gaps:

- managers did not have an accurate perception of customer expectations;
- those perceptions held by managers were not fully translated into a service package specification;
- the service package actually delivered did not match the specification;
- there was a failure to communicate the service delivery process to customers;
- as a result the service package desired by the customer was not that which they actually received (Parasuraman *et al.*, 1985).

More recently research into local authority housing management illustrates the way in which measures of customers' satisfaction may give a false impression of the match between delivered and desired service packages. Figure 2.5 plots the relationship between tenants' net satisfaction with aspects of the housing authority's service package and the importance they ascribe to each element. It illustrates that while there is high satisfaction with some elements they are not perceived as being of great importance. Conversely there is little net satisfaction with a number of service aspects which are particularly important to cutomers. The use of such a grid can provide an important device for prioritising action on service quality particularly where resources are scarce (see Chapter 9).

Figure 2.5: Tenant satisfaction and priorities in the housing service

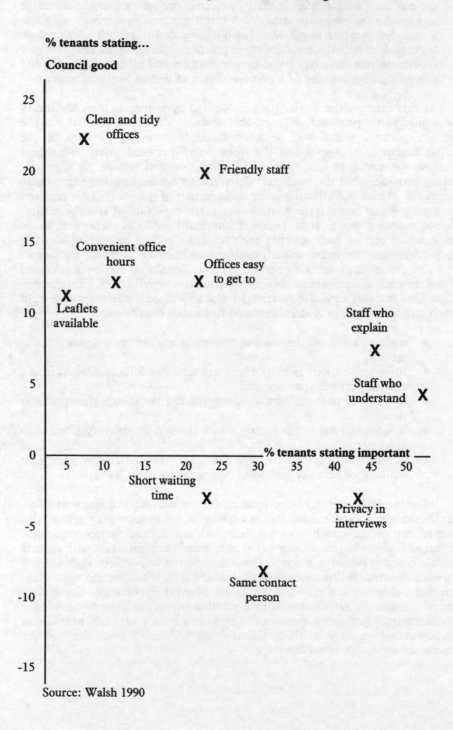

% tenants stating...

Council good

25

X   Clean and tidy offices

20   X   Friendly staff

15

Convenient office hours

X   Offices easy to get to

X   X

X
Leaflets
available   Staff who
10   explain

X

Staff who
understand   X

5

0 _____ % tenants stating important __

  5   10   15   20   25   30   35   40   45   50

Short waiting
time   X   X
                              Privacy in
-5   interviews

X
Same contact
person
-10

-15

Source: Walsh 1990

Constraints on service quality

Because local government is directly elected and has the provision of services to the public as a central purpose, a customer orientation has often been assumed rather than demonstrated. There are, however, important constraints on service quality which are reflected in the external relationship of the local authority to its customers as well as its internal operation.

External relationships

Not knowing what customers want. Local authorities have well developed systems for collecting and analysing social, economic and demographic data, yet little use has been made of public opinion and market research methodologies to provide a qualitative picture of customers' needs or evaluation of service quality. Until recently consultation and participation exercises were infrequent and not always designed to enable customers' full involvement. As a result, producer (and particularly professional) interpretations have dominated in the design of services, for example through professional standards and a lack of thought about the design of forms, and the customer's direct expression of need or evaluation of services has rarely been heard. Where customers were vocal in expressing their views it was usually in opposition to a proposal – a school closure, new road scheme or housing redevelopment. Being essentially reactive and often lacking the resources to suggest viable alternatives their views could be easily dismissed as 'parochial' or 'biased' and hence disregarded by the local authority.

Not saying what's available. The provision of information was also not well developed. Local authorities became producer rather than customer-oriented because they were supplying monopoly or near-monopoly services and therefore seldom had to think about attracting or retaining customers. Where services involved eligibility criteria or rationing procedures the information provided tended to be complex and detailed – often written from the perspective of bureaucratic defensiveness than assisting customers. Finally the organisational complexity of all but small local authorities and the large number of service delivery points meant that the customer would often find that the information and facilities to meet the range of their needs was not available from a single source.

Limiting access. In addition to limits on information there are other constraints on customers' access to services. Some services tended to be centralised rather than provided at neighbourhood level, physical access to buildings was not always easy for people with prams or mobility difficulties, the environment in waiting areas and offices could be uncomfortable and intimidating, translation facilities were seldom available for customers whose main language was not English and offices operated on a 9 to 5 day when evenings or weekends could be the easiest time for some customers. Access to decision-making and the design of services was limited to the local election process, the occasional *ad hoc* consultation or being part of a pressure group which had managed to gain the local authority's ear.

Variable service delivery. Service delivery itself was variable. Customers might experience excellent schools or leisure centres, but wait weeks to be assessed for a home help or have a pot-hole in their street repaired. Council house tenants, a group of customers with limited alternative suppliers, have consistently suffered from a poor repairs service yet have had little opportunity to obtain redress. While some of the explanation can be attributed to central government constraint on local expenditure this is not the whole picture. Poor management and working practices together with the local political context have all contributed to services which put producer interests before those of customers and have failed to tackle deficiencies in service delivery.

Internal operation

Not measuring services on customers' criteria. The measurement of organisational performance in local government has been dominated by indicators which have little to do with the direct experience of customers (Figure 2.6). Even the main customer-based indicator, public support and voting behaviour at local election time, is of limited use since many authorities hold elections one year in four, a considerable proportion of seats are 'safe' and party loyalty over-rides even the poor quality service citizens sometimes receive from their local authority. Traditionally the key management indicator has been expenditure. During the 1960s and 1970s local authorities became machines for spending and the assumption that additional expenditure leads to better quality service is still strong – although recently this has declined as a result of value-for-money methodologies being introduced. In the last decade a range of other performance indicators have been developed although these tend to be related to the resources under the organisation's control, for example the cost per user or capacity utilised, rather than reflecting the customer-based quality measures discussed earlier.

Figure 2.6: Customer and local authority measures of performance

The local authority asks . . .
- how many employees per 1,000 population?
- numbers of applications processed?
- what is the cost per user?
- how many empty properties?
- what underspend in the budget?

while the customer asks . . .
- will I have to take time off work to visit the council offices?
- will the phone be engaged?
- can I get what I want?
- how long will I have to wait?
- will there be something for my children to do in the waiting room?

Not giving quality service within the authority. The structure and culture of the management (as opposed to political) side of the local authority tends to be based firmly on the Weberian model of bureaucracy. It is hierarchical, functionally differentiated (often on the basis of professional areas of specialism) and rule-bound. Conformity with statute or the authority's policy, which may not have been reviewed for some time, are significant limitations on the development of a customer-oriented culture. Managers are almost universally recruited from the professional specialism for which they will be responsible as there is no tradition of general management. They therefore bring with them a set of norms about best professional practice which may not always accord with their customers' own perceptions. The department, the basic unit for service delivery, therefore has a strong pre-disposition towards producer views and interests. Inevitably, such a bureaucratic structure has strong internal divisions between functional areas, a tension compounded by heightened competition for resources. These organisational issues act as constraints on meeting those customer needs which do not fit organisational boundaries. For example, effective service provision for children under five years of age requires integration between social services, education, libraries and other departments – yet this customer group may not be given the same priority in each part of the organisation because of varying political or professional interests (see Chapter 7).

Approaches to service quality

Earlier it was argued that for local authorities to treat someone as a customer involved according them greater power as well as changing the assumptions underlying the design and delivery of services. In other words it involves questions of customers' power over and above their basic rights as citizens as well as the organisation's service orientation. These two dimensions form a matrix which illustrate the different forms of relationship between customer and local authority and hence different approaches to service quality (Figure 2.7).

The bottom left-hand quadrant, where customer power is limited and service assumptions are paternalistic, represents *bureaucratic paternalism* (Hambleton *et al.*, 1989). Here the local authority is closed to the voices of its customers, unresponsive because of its rule-bound and hierarchical nature and makes decisions on the belief that it alone knows best. *Customer care*, in the bottom right-hand quadrant, is exemplified by authorities engaging in initiatives designed to improve the quality of the service relationships and the physical setting. In her review of customer approaches in the health service Winkler (1987, p.1) has termed this the 'supermarket approach' because it is about 'customer relations, not patients' rights'. Notably absent from customer care, therefore, is any substantial shift in the power balance. *Community power* is a situation where customers exercise extensive power over the nature and type of services, but the assumptions underlying the way the authority meets these remains paternalistic. For example a tenants' association could be given a budget to fund environmental improvements on an estate but still experience considerable difficulty in obtaining a swift and effective housing repairs service. The authority has increased customers' choice, but made no attempt to develop its own service orientation. Finally, in the top right quadrant, *customer service* combines extensive customer power with strategies to improve service quality. Here the authority seeks to address

Figure 2.7: Maping local authority approaches to service quality

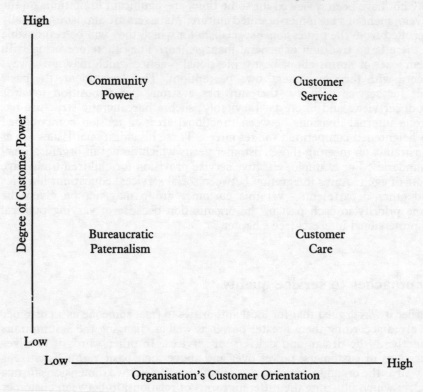

all four groups of factors which customers use to evaluate service quality (see Figure 2.3).

The concern with putting customers first involves local authorities moving away from bureaucratic paternalism and in doing this many have developed customer care as an alternative. Redesign of reception areas, improved information provision and training of front-line employees are all hallmarks of this approach. Some have ventured into community power, particularly though the creation of community councils and customer involvement in decision-making. Others are now engaged in developing models of customer service, including working with specific sets of customers to codify their rights, formulating and publicising customer contracts and consultation with customers to review and redesign services. These strategies are discussed in greater detail in Chapters 3, 5 and 6.

Developing a customer orientation

Reorientating local authorities to adopt a customer focus and concentrate on service quality is a major task. It requires the questioning and review of accepted procedures and change in the culture of the organisation. Yet it is precisely the task that increasing numbers of authorities set themselves and in which important and significant strides are being made. At a time of rapid and major change for local government and severe limits on financial and human resources this is no mean achievement.

Devoting this early chapter to exploring who local authority customers are, the ways in which they evaluate service quality and the constraints which local authorities need to overcome is designed to ensure that these individuals are at the forefront as more detailed issues of managing for service quality are considered.

3 Reviewing services

Service review is essential in any strategy to improve quality and the process should fully involve those who receive and deliver services. In the words of the facilitator of one large consultation exercise:

> Internal local authority concerns and professional views are so much a part of our way of working that it is easy for customer perceptions to slip from view almost without us noticing. It requires constant effort to pull customer concerns to the centre of debate and action (Webster 1990, p.21).

While there are examples of research and analysis being undertaken without concomitant improvements in quality, the converse will be rare. Local authorities cannot develop service quality without a clear understanding of:

- customers' evaluations of existing services;
- current and future needs of customers;
- issues facing employees in delivering services;
- political values and priorities;
- professional, managerial and legislative developments;
- the resource context.

Professional bodies, management training, technical journals and contacts with colleagues and elected members all help to keep officers informed. However there is often limited information available at management level about the experience of customers and their needs and priorities or the issues for employees in carrying out council policy and delivering services. Because of the hierarchical structure and culture of the local authority and managers' infrequent direct contact with customers important data is not readily available without a conscious effort being made to collect it.

There are a range of available and tested methods which can be employed to overcome this deficiency. Market research, consultation and other forms of direct data collection can be supplemented by analysis of existing information sources, for example on waiting lists, complaints or demographic structure. Focus groups and related approaches to qualitative research provide a means of gaining important insights into customers' experiences and perceptions and may be used as the basis for designing questionnaires from a user perspective. Several authorities have central or departmental research and marketing units who undertake this role while others commission studies from consultants or higher education institutes.

This chapter discusses the ways in which local authorities can review services from a customer perspective. It uses a number of terms – need, demand, equality – which are discussed further in the next chapter. Consultation with and information collection from employees are dealt with more fully in Chapter 8.

Finding out from customers – the key questions

As with any type of research local authorities need to ask themselves a number of questions before embarking on an activity to find out from customers. The key questions are:

- What is the purpose of this work? The authority should have a clear and specific formulation of the problem that it wants to investigate and the objectives of the research in order that the study can be designed to provide the data required.
- Is the data already available? There are a large number of data collection activities in any local authority. Some will be regular formalised processes while others will be *ad hoc* and irregular. Some or all of the data required may already be available.
- Has anyone else already undertaken this type of study? Check with other local authorities and agencies (for example the health authority) to see whether similar work has been undertaken and what lessons can be applied. Professional and local government networks can be used, for example the local authority associations, Local Authority Research and Intelligence Network, the Local Government Management Board's Training and Management Information Service, the INLOGOV/DoE register of research and academic institutions.
- Should customers, consultants or in-house expertise be used to undertake the research? Customers already have knowledge of services and if involved in the design or conduct of a study may be able to obtain a more accurate and detailed picture than council officials. There may be consultants with experience in the field the authority requires who will also be able to provide comparative data to supplement the results as well as a pool of trained interviewers. The authority may have sufficient research expertise in-house or decide to employ consultants solely to undertake the questionnaire design and fieldwork stages. Employees in customer contact roles provide an important resource and could be involved in undertaking the research.
- Can the cost be shared with another agency? Where the research involves a short questionnaire it may be possible to combine with another survey being undertaken in the area thus reducing the costs of the fieldwork stage.
- How are the results to be presented? Undertaking a survey or consultation exercise with customers and citizens is a public statement by the authority of a desire to find out what people think and what

they would like the authority to do as a result. It is important to consider the form in which the results are to be released as this too will reflect on the customer's perception of the authority's service quality and commitment to change.

● What will happen once the results are available? The research must be used positively to improve service quality. Local authorities should therefore have a clear mechanism for analysing the results, determining the changes required and implementing them. There needs to be a firm link into the policy process of the organisation.

In *Learning From the Public* (LGMB 1989) a series of aims and appoaches to finding out from customers and citizens are outlined (Figure 3.1). The types of methods fall into three main groups:

● direct research using surveys and market research with customers;
● indirect research through analysis of existing data;
● consultation with and participation of customers and citizens.

Direct research with customers

Surveys are the most common form of direct information collection and have been used by local authorities over many years. Until recently, however, they tended solely to be concerned with gathering data on environmental issues rather than customer attitudes and opinions. House condition and road traffic surveys provided valuable data but were seldom also used to discover what customers thought of the authority's housing or transportation policies – or what they wanted from the organisation. A major advance in recent years has been to use surveys to build a clearer picture of customers' and citizens' attitudes, opinions and preferences. A number of different models are now being used.

● General customer satisfaction surveys. These seek to identify levels of satisfaction and dissatisfaction with the local authority and its services on the basis of a survey of a sample of residents. They provide a general picture of public attitudes and can form the basis for more detailed research.
● Surveys of specific customer groups. A similar approach can be used with specific customer groups, for example council house tenants or women. This will provide a more detailed picture of attitudes, preferences and needs.
● Surveys on specific issues. The authority may commission a survey on an issue of local concern prior to the development or review of its policy. Newham LB commissioned a survey on issues of crime and safety in the borough which revealed that particular groups in the community were discouraged from making use of council facilities because of a fear of harassment and street attack.
● Regular surveys. While a one-off survey can be useful, repeat surveys provide an opportunity to track changes in customer attitudes, monitor the effect of initiatives designed to improve service quality and identify new issues. When undertaken on a regular basis every year

Figure 3.1: Finding out from customers – aims and approaches

Aim	Information about	Methods
1. To formulate policy make decisions and allocate resources	Customers' preferences Need for services Future needs Suggestions from the public	Surveys Consultation Statistics on demand, usage, demography Surveys Group discussions with users/non-users Liaison with voluntary sector Trend analysis of data Suggestion schemes Community forums Community/user decision making
2. To monitor performance	Satisfaction/dissatisfaction Specific problems Experience of minority/disadvantaged groups	Surveys Community monitoring Monitoring by user groups Complaints monitoring Monitoring members' surgeries and ward contacts Consultation with groups/individuals Advocacy schemes
3. To develop the authority's links	Public attitudes to the authority/service Difficulties of customer/citizens in communicating with the authority Improving the relationship	Market research Discussions with focus group or citizens' panel Surveys Service sampling Free 'phones, hot lines All methods that establish a dialogue Responding actively to suggestions and complaints
4. To transfer choices and power to customers and communities	What choices do people want? Giving users/communities choice and power	Surveys Group discussions Public consultation Examine patterns of use Local budgets and committees

Source: Adapted from LGMB 1989

or two they provide an importance source of information on trends in customer attitudes. Cleveland CC has conducted a residents' survey regularly since the late 1970s.

Quantitative survey techniques are good at providing an overall assessment but have a major limitation since questions tend to be structured in terms of the services and activities of the authority. As a result they fail to provide information on needs and wants which are not reflected in the existing pattern of service or the cumulative impact of council activities on the customer. This latter point is particularly important for the authority concerned to improve service quality. Customers' opportunities and choices are frequently shaped and influenced by the interaction of a number of council policies and services rather than by discrete encounters. Finding out from customers involves finding out about the interactions between services – the way in which the absence of supervised child-care for two or three hours after school prevents a customer from caring for an elderly relative on the way home from work; or how poor street lighting and a failure to remove racist graffiti may heighten the concerns of black women about their safety and discourage them from attending women-only events offered at a leisure centre in the evening. Uncovering the effects of council policy and practice, which often remain hidden from the authority, is the basis for making real progress on the quality of service.

Qualitative methods are now increasingly employed, often forming an integral part of a research methodology which also employs quantitative surveys. They frequently take the form of a group discussion, although a number of different models are available:

- a discussion with a group of customers to test out the issues to be included in a quantitative survey;
- convening a representative panel of residents at which existing services can be discussed and new developments explored prior to a decision being made;
- meeting with existing community-based forums – tenants' associations, pre-school play groups, churches and temples;
- bringing together a specific group of customers to explore issues of concern to them in relation to local authority activity or inactivity – older people, small businesses, teenagers, voluntary organisations;
- bringing together users of one service – leisure centre, allotment or meals-on-wheels users.

There are now a number of examples of this approach:

- Gloucestershire CC used a variety of methods to review and redesign provision for the under fives. A postal survey of 1000 parents with children under five was conducted by the social service department's research officer. The health authority provided listings of parents in return for the council including some additional questions. The response rate was 70 per cent. 28 local consultation meetings with parents were held to discuss the issues identified and explore options. A councillor and an officer attended each. Both day and evening meetings were held, with a creche provided at the former. Consultation meetings with staff and other interested parties were also organised.

- Prior to their survey of attitudes towards council services Hammersmith and Fulham LB organised panel discussions with representative groups of residents from different areas of the borough. Additional meetings were held with specific groups including unemployed people, Asian women, elderly women in sheltered accommodation and mothers. The results of these discussions led to revisions in the questionnaire as well as providing data for the final report.

Indirect research

Indirect research involves utilising the data which is already available about customers and their behaviour rather than going out and asking them. The Census provides an obvious source, as do other nationally produced statistics on such aspects as unemployment, economic activity and morbidity and mortality. Audit Commission profiles can provide another source. This data can be used to assess current policies and levels of service against changes in the environment; for example, are economic development, adult education and recreation services responding to changes in the unemployment rate and do they match the characteristics of unemployed people? Often this will involve the definition of benchmarks against which provision can be reviewed, for example skill training places per 1000 unemployed people.

- Birmingham City Council Women's Unit produced a review of demographic and social changes affecting women. It explored the impact of household formation, population structure and labour market changes, as well as childcare, transport and other barriers to women's employment. Implications for council policy were highlighted.

The local authority will also have its own statistics, for example:

- utilisation against capacity;
- waiting lists;
- waiting times;
- complaints recorded;
- call-outs requested;
- praise received;
- applications received;
- appeals registered;
- educational attainment of pupils and students;
- enquiries made;
- numbers attending;
- length of visit;

and so on. Monitoring these against specified standards and over time will give an indication of the authority's performance and customers' attitudes.

For example:

A museum in an area with a long established Asian community monitored the number and type of visitors. This revealed that it had very few Asian visitors. On reviewing the service it became clear that one reason was the lack of any exhibits or information on that community and its contribution to the city.

Analysis of such data provide an indicator of matters which require direct research with customers.

Consultation

As local authorities have begun to apply the ideas of service quality so interest in consultation with customers has developed. Consultation is one of the forms of active relationship between local authority and customers and citizens (Figure 3.2). Consultation is defined as customer or citizen involvement in the exploration of issues and choices. In other words, it involves more than a marginal degree of power on the part of customers or citizens.

Figure 3.2: Forms of active relationship between customers and local authority

Information → Opinion → Discussion → Customer/ → Joint → Decisions
provision   surveys   of local   citizen   decision   devolved to
by local   authority   exploration   making   customers/
authority   proposals   of issues   citizens
                                         and choices

Establishing consultation requires careful thought and an ability to see things from the customer's or citizen's perspective. Is is usually undertaken through meetings:

A local authority wanted to consult with the residents of an area. After obtaining a list of community organisations it invited them to send representatives to a meeting in the hall of the local primary school to 'discuss the future of your neighbourhood'. The meeting was chaired from the stage by a ward councillor and consisted of presentations by officers from the planning, highways and housing departments on their analysis of the issues facing the neighbourhood. The representatives were then invited to ask questions and express their views. Discussion consisted of points being raised by members of the audience and answered by council officers in terms of their ideas for the area. The exception was when questions were asked about the future of the school if it opted out of local authority control, an issue of some concern locally which no-one from the authority was qualified to answer. The discussion soon ground to a halt as, after listening to 45 minutes of officer presentation which contained few visual aids and much technical language, the representatives were feeling uncomfortable on the pupil-sized chairs they were required to use. The meeting concluded with a rather confused process to nominate two representatives who would liaise with the officers on future developments. The officers and councillor departed feeling that they had not learnt anything they did not already know, but had done their duty. The representatives went away feeling that they had not really been listened to and that the council already knew what it wanted to do with the area. They also felt that the agenda had been set by the council and that their concerns, especially over the school, were not addressed. Leaving, one local shop-keeper commented: 'I probably haven't lost a lot of money coming to this meeting, but it would have been nice if they'd at least appreciated the time we've given up and maybe offered us a cup of coffee!'. In the next issue of the local paper there was a letter from some young people who wanted better youth facilities asking why they had not been invited to the meeting. The liaison group met a couple of times in the evenings, but was wound up after the two nominees started giving their apologies.

This example highlights a number of lessons for those embarking on consultation exercises (Figure 3.3).

Figure 3.3: Guidelines for consultation

- Be clear what the consultation is about.
- Have a process for responding to issues which are raised but fall outside the formal agenda.
- Make sure that all interests are able to be represented.
- Recognise which voices tend to be heard and which not.
- Make the meetings customer friendly.
- Be clear with customers and citizens about the process following the consultation.
- Be open about the resource limitations.
- Be realistic about the amount of time people will devote to being involved.
- Do not treat people, even if elected from a consultation meeting, as experts on or representatives of 'their' group.
- Keep the member and officer role to the minimum.

It is essential for the authority to make it clear what the consultation is about. In the case study the representatives thought that they were being invited to discuss any issues to do with the area, while the local authority only wanted to look at environmental issues. Yet even where the local authority is clear about its agenda this may not reflect the community's concerns. The ability to collectively establish and negotiate the agenda and to respond to customers' and citizens' priorities is an essential hallmark of good consultation practice.

Because local authorities traditionally have not engaged in consultation exercises groups see this as a key means to exercise influence and those who are excluded feel this keenly. Steps should be taken to ensure that all interests are able to be represented. Some interests are not organised into formal groups, like the young people in the example. Others may not be able to attend due to the time of the meeting or the lack of accessibility of its location. It may, for instance, not be on a bus route or have access for people with a physical disability. The provision of a creche can also be important, especially for daytime meetings, as can appropriate support to any deaf or blind people wishing to attend.

Some voices in the community tend to be heard by the local authority and others not. Business interests or tenants' associations, for example, may have much easier access to officers and members than other groups. Additionally the culture of the local authority will contain a view of those groups who 'have a contribution to make', are 'realistic' and whom 'we can work with', and of those who are 'out to cause trouble' and 'always playing the same tune'. These views are often stereotypical and therefore may not match the reality. It is important to identify those groups that the local authority or political process marginalises and establish specific consultation opportunities for them. For example, this might involve establishing a young person's forum or a consultation programme with gypsies and travellers. Additionally the local authority should not treat people, even if elected from a consultation meeting, as experts on or representatives of 'their' group. The community may have put them there to keep an eye on the local authority rather than to be the reference point the council would prefer. It is important to check back with the wider constituency at appropriate points rather than place two or three people in the difficult position of being the community's unofficial spokespeople.

The local authority must be realistic about the amount of time people will devote to being involved. Officers are paid, councillors are elected but residents become involved because they have an interest in the issues. Few will be willing to devote large amounts of time to consultation exercises – they have other priorities in their lives. For those who are being asked to make a special contribution, expenses and some form of payment should be offered. Training and other appropriate support may be necessary.

The consultation should be something people enjoy, feel is worthwhile and would be willing to attend again. Meetings should be customer friendly with the organisers making it easy for people to contribute and not expecting them to sit for long periods listening to experts. Workshops or small discussion groups can be used so that ideas can be explored in a more intimate setting and then reported back to the larger meeting. Participants' needs and comfort must be thought about. Regular breaks can be provided and refreshment offered. Running a consultation meeting like a local authority committee will not be a successful or rewarding experience for any of the participants.

People attending a consultation event are contributing to a process and will want to know what happens next. It is important that the local authority is clear with customers and citizens about the whole process and what will happen after their involvement. Too often the results seem to disappear into the local authority with little indication of their effect on subsequent decisions. This discourages people from taking part in future consultations since they feel it has been of little real value. The local authority should also be open about the resource limitations. People's expectations tend to be raised when the authority is unclear or vague about the resources available. Sometimes this will be caused by officers or councillors not wishing to give news they feel will be unpopular. However the experience of consultation is that people do know that resources are scarce and can take this on board. They may at the same time take political action to increase the level of resources available.

Finally the member and officer role in consultation with customers and citizens must be kept to the minimum. It can be intimidating and disempowering to be confronted by a group of apparently confident, intelligent and well qualified experts. The role of officers in particular should be confined to giving essential information and assisting people attending the consultation to contribute as effectively as possible. Consultation meetings are an opportunity for customers and citizens to be heard. Professionals and other employees, as well as members, should have separate channels.

A number of good practice examples of consultation are now emerging.

- Coventry Social Services Department undertook a review of services to people with physical disabilities. A key element was consultation with people with disabilities and their carers. Recognising the variety of needs and interests, a series of meetings were held with day care users, people with a learning difficulty, older people with physical disabilities, children with special needs, people with a learning difficulty and a physical disability and a range of other groups. While the lead officer at each meeting was given a list of issues that might be covered, they were requested to use this to ensure a wide-ranging discussion and to encourage additional points to be raised. A clear set of ground-rules were also published (Figure 3.4). Consultation with professionals, other agencies and other service providers was organised separately.

- In a number of local authorities ongoing consultation processes with black and minority ethnic communities have been established. In Tameside a black women's group has developed, bringing together black women council employees with members of the three main Asian communities in the area. Meetings started in the council offices but soon moved to more familiar locations in the community. Chairing of the group rotates and training and support is provided both to women employees and members of the community. Interpretation is conducted informally and refreshments are always provided. The group has initiated discussions with council departments and developed links with other forums for black people and women (Yusuf and Kettleborough 1990).

Quality audits – a model for service reviews

Quality audits have been developed by several local authorities and provide a comprehensive method of reviewing services which fully involve customers and employees in the process. The Labour Party has adopted quality audits within its policy for local government and it is intended they will overcome the limitations of value for money studies by focussing on value for people.

Figure 3.4: Ground-rules for a consultation exercise

1. All people with a disability have the right to contribute to the consultation meeting and each person should speak for his or her self. If a person is unable to speak then an advocate can speak on their behalf.
2. The named carer of a person with a disability has the right to contribute to the consultation meeting and each one should speak for his or herself.
3. People who are unable to attend meetings but have a disability or are the named carer of a disabled person have the right to contribute to the consultation by letter.
4. Professionals from the local authority or the health authority may attend meetings as observers or facilitators.
5. Professionals at meetings have no right to contribute to the consultation meeting.
6. The consultation exists to enable users influence in the future planning of services; no promises can be made in advance about the future pattern of service provision.
7. No service providers should be criticised by name.
8. No statements made by users or carers will be recorded as attributable to the individual who made them.
9. Personal issues raised in the group workshops remain confidential to that group unless the individual wishes to raise the issue with the whole meeting.
10. The chairperson will pursue any personal issues raised that require attention.
11. All the findings of each consultation meeting will be reported back to the people attending or contributing by letter.
12. The people contributing to the meeting have the right to amend the report should they believe it to be an inaccurate record of the meeting.

Source: Coventry Social Services Department 1990

Two of the authorities who have pioneered quality audits are York and Islington. In York a pilot audit of the swimming pools service included:

- a survey of customer opinions on the service, including levels of satisfaction and dissatisfaction;
- a survey of non-users undertaken across the catchment area of each pool;
- customer/employee panels to identify in greater detail the issues for each pool and how service quality could be improved;
- an analysis of operational performance in terms of economy and efficiency.

A quality audit team was established consisting of officers from leisure services department and the policy and performance, marketing and communications and personnel units. The quality audit provided the basis for preparing for CCT in leisure management.

Islington has also established interdepartmental quality audit teams. The agenda for each team covers:

- Service standards – identifying and assessing those that exist, the way they are monitored and how they are communicated to the public, managers and members.
- Comparative service levels – a statistical analysis of provision, staffing and expenditure in relation to comparable authorities.
- Policy effectiveness – establishing whether policy is being implemented as intended and is achieving its desired effect.
- Equality – assessing the appropriateness of service standards in terms of the nature of the community and the equality dimension of service delivery and accessibility.
- Consumer satisfaction – using quantitative and qualitative mechanisms, including consultation.
- Finance – assessing value for money and financial mangement and control systems.
- Human resources – evaluating the level and deployment of human resources, working relationships and practices and personnel management.

Quality audits are being undertaken on neighbourhood office reception and the meals on wheels service amongst others.

The aim of quality audits is to build the fullest possible picture of the current service, customer needs and requirements, employee views on ways of improving service and the use of resources. Underlying this approach is the recognition that service reviews by managers alone or analyses concentrating purely on financial questions are inevitably partial. Auditing for quality involves considering financial and managerial perspectives but should also include the range of other issues and views.

Developing service review

Service review is an indispensable part of the process of developing service quality. It should provide the local authority with a clearer view of the environment within which it is operating, customer evaluations of existing services and their preferences for the future. In the absence of this baseline local authorities may be able to redesign services in ways which they believe will improve quality, but will not know whether their view is shared by customers. The range of approaches discussed in this chapter therefore provide a means of evaluating and redesigning services with service quality in mind.

4 Key elements in service review and design

In service review processes terms such as needs, efficiency and equality are often used but seldom defined in clear or unambiguous terms. Understanding what these concepts mean and how they can be applied in practical ways is more than just an intellectual exercise. It is fundamental to the ability of local authorities to develop effective review methodologies and design high quality services. A narrow definition of need, for example, can preclude the consideration of other important data. Equality too has a variety of meanings which bear on the specification of services and their ability to reach various groups of customers.

This chapter defines and identifies the practical implications of using a number of key concepts in service review and design:

- need and demand;
- equality and discrimination;
- economy, efficiency and effectiveness;
- rationing.

It then outlines seven alternative principles upon which services can be organised and explores the consequences of adopting each.

Need and demand

Local authorities have often sought to define need in objective terms by reference to professional, bureaucratic or legal standards. These include:

- number of children;
- level of income;
- distance from school;
- places per 1000 members of the client group;
- extent of disability;
- length of residence.

These can then be distinguished from individuals' subjectively defined wants. For example:

An individual may *want* more housing benefit because they feel that their income is inadequate, but the local authority (acting on behalf of central government) will respond that they do not *need* it because they are already receiving the correct level in terms of statutory provision.

To the customer this may seem more like a means of rationing services than objectively assessing need, and rightly so since bureaucratic and professional standards vary over time as resource levels and opinions about public policies change and develop. Additionally not all standards are objectively identifiable. Despite the development of explicit assessment systems, for example in allocating home help services, many require interpretation by a service provider hopefully (but not inevitably) on the basis of professional or other training. They therefore have an element of subjectivity.

As a result of these issues four different ways of defining needs are used (Figure 4.1). *Expressed need* is an indicator of people's personal identification of their requirement for a service. The need will be expressed through using or applying for the service, for example going swimming or requesting that their child is statemented, or by public campaigns, pressure group activity and contacts with councillors or officers. The great strength of this indicator is that it is a tangible demonstration of people's requirements and feelings. It does however have two major limitations. It is partial in the sense that not everyone may know about the service or be able to gain access to it, nor may campaigns be representative of community views. Secondly the expression of views and decision to apply for a service will be influenced by people's perception of the outcome. If they do not believe that they will get the service they may decide not to bother applying.

Felt need is established through a more systematic enquiry into people's situation, perception and preferences. A department may conduct interviews or group discussions to establish whether people feel they need a new or different service. Consultation exercises (see Chapter 3) are examples of techniques to identify felt need. Inquiries into felt need can be designed to ensure that the views heard are representative of the customer group or groups involved. They should, for example, cover users as well as non-users of a service. The difficulty is that unless customers are also presented with meaningful resource information they are not able to give a full indication of their preferences. People need to be aware of the financial and other costs and benefits associated with their decisions in order to give an informed view.

Rather than relying on people's actual behaviour or feelings need can be defined authoritatively. *Normative* need refers to a standard or criteria which a local authority applies uniformly to a class of customers or citizens. There are many examples of this including:

- housing allocation systems;
- discounts for young people in swimming pools;
- formula arrangements for allocating resources to schools or other decentralised outlets (see Chapter 7); and
- first come, first served appointment systems.

A normative definition of need can be useful from a bureaucratic point of view. It may allow a committee or authority to bid for more resources if it can demonstrate that there is substantial unmet need. In mid 1991, for example, social service authorities bid for additional resources by arguing that

Figure 4.1: Definitions of need

Criteria of need	Characteristics	Strengths	Weaknesses	Methods of analysis
Expressed	Tangible behaviour and actions	Easy to identify	Partial Service must already exist	Usage Surveys
Felt	Personal wants and desires	Representative May reveal hidden expressed needs	May not take costs into account	Consultation Interviews
Normative	Authoritatively defined	Explicit Uniformly applied	Does not take individual preferences into account May vary with resources	Bureaucratic, political and professional decisions
Comparative	With reference to other providers/customers	Basis for identifying areas requiring further investigation	Casual link may be tenuous Organisational factors may influence apparent need	Comparative statistics

Developed from Clayton 1983.

the lack of qualifications and formal training on the part of staff in residential homes for children resulted in poor service quality. The difficulty for the customer is that this definition of need varies as the resource and political climate changes. In periods of resource famine the definition of need for local authority nursery places has tightened in order to further restrict the numbers eligible. It also permits the local authority to reject expressed and felt need on the basis that these are subjective definitions while normative need is apparently objective and impartially applied. This further restricts the customer's voice in determining the nature and level of service.

Comparative need also rests on apparently objective criteria. It has two different elements. Firstly comparative need may be established by examining the level of provision in one authority against that in another, standardised for demographic structure, economic profile and other relevant variables. If the level of provision in the base authority is lower than the average it could be argued that there was a level of comparative need and hence that provision should be increased. This approach to defining need can be a quick and useful way of identifying areas where more detailed investigations are required.

The second way in which comparative need can be identified is through establishing the characteristics of those currently receiving the service and assuming that all with similar characteristics also need it. If:

(a)   the size of the total population having these characteristics, and
(b)   the proportion receiving the service are known

it is possible to identify the amount of comparative and by implication unmet need. This approach is more applicable to some services than others. The main limitation is the assumed causal connection between the characteristics of the service recipients and the need of non-recipients also with those characteristics. Just because residents of elderly persons' homes tend to be over 70, have a physical disability and are single does not mean that similar individuals need the service. They may require some support but perhaps would prefer it in a different form. The danger of using comparative need as an indicator is therefore that it takes the existing method of service provision as given. Additionally policy change can influence the characteristics of users. For example:

A local authority wishes to ensure 100 per cent capacity utilisation of facilities in order to maximise income and achieve economy of scale benefits. When demand for the facility falls the eligibility criteria are relaxed and hence the characteristics of users change.

This process has been identified in the way in which some sheltered housing schemes are managed. Comparative need indicators may therefore say more about the policy of the organisation than the needs of customers and citizens.

The concept *demand* is often used to refer to expressed need, for example the housing waiting list indicates the 'demand' for accommodation. Its correct usage, however, is by incorporating cost into the equation. No public service provision is cost free. Instead of trying to identify how much people need, therefore, perhaps the question to ask is: what price is the individual prepared or able to pay for the service?

Payment can be made in two ways: through taxation or charging systems. Some local authorities have conducted public opinion surveys which have asked people to express their preferences between different levels of services and rates/poll tax. Asking people how much they would be prepared to pay for services which are collectively consumed or regulatory (for example, roads and planning control) or are largely financed through the general tax system are hypothetical and of limited value. However it is possible to establish useful data on demand where services are subject to a charge. This might involve surveys of users or monitoring the effects of price changes where the service specification remains constant, for example increasing car park charges. In this case it is important to distinguish between *effective* and *latent* demand. The former refers to a situation where individuals have the resources to purchase services, for example to use a leisure centre. If an individual who was on a low income wanted to use the leisure centre but did not have the necessary resources to pay the entrance charges this would be referred to as latent demand. Local authorities have responded to latent demand through concessionary fees schemes such as the passport to leisure which provides free or cut-price access to facilities.

Because many local government services do not have a direct charge to the user it is difficult to apply this approach on a widespread basis. Additionally charges have different purposes:

- Some, such as adult education, exist because the local authority has decided that it is right that individuals should contribute financially towards a service, although this may or may not be on a full-cost basis.
- Other charges may be a penalty, for example fines on overdue books.
- Finally charges may be imposed to ration demand. One example would be differential pricing on parking meters depending on their relative closeness to the city centre.

Using the concept of demand in service review would therefore involve the local authority explicitly considering the resource allocation preferences of individuals and groups, while recognising that for some disposable income and choice are constrained – the elderly disabled person whose sole source of income is a state pension may have little choice but to use the meals-on-wheels service.

Quality and equality

Quality and equality are intimately connected. While the development of service quality involves thinking about the customer as an individual it is also essential to recognise that they are members of particular groups, defined in terms of their sex, ethnic origin, age, physical ability or other characteristics. The customer may therefore be discriminated against in the type of service they receive or the way it is delivered as a direct consequence of their group membership.

Quality and Equality (LGMB 1991) points out that a failure to consider questions of equality as an integral part of service improvement initiatives means that the local authority is making a number of assumptions:

- assuming the service provided meets the needs of all groups of customers – as a result of failing to identify and differentiate between various groups;
- assuming that the needs and membership of particular groups are uniform and discrete – by ignoring the fact that customers do not fall into mutually exclusive groups;
- assuming that services do not discriminate – by maintaining the line that 'everyone is treated equally' without collecting data to support this or monitor whether there is equality of outcome (see below);
- assuming uniform methods can discover customers' views – by not designing the survey or consultation with the needs of various customers in mind;
- assuming that one form of information provision is suitable for all customers – by not recognising, for example, the various languages or physical abilities of customers;
- assuming that the organisation operates in an environment where all views and opinions are heard and taken into account – by failing to recognise the local authority's selectivity in who it listens to and what priority it accords that information (see Chapter 6);
- assuming that the composition of the local authority's employees has no effect on service quality – by failing to recognise the value a varied workforce brings to an understanding of the community and the ability to deliver services responsively and sensitively;
- assuming that services can be managed or evaluated without involving those who receive them, deliver them or would like to make use of them – by believing that customers and employees have little to offer.

Where local authorities make these assumptions or permit them to continue unchallenged they will be lessening the impact of their commitment to quality and failing to take the opportunity to redress inequalities.

Equality

Equality in local government services can be assessed in a number of ways:

- Equality of public expenditure – that expenditure on a service should be allocated equally between customers. This could be undertaken on a simple *pro rata* basis but more appropriately would take need into account (see Chapter 3).
- Equality of access – that each individual has the same degree of access to services or facilities as another, taking access in the widest sense to include cost as well as physical and geographical factors. The location of neighbourhood offices provides an example. The criteria might be that all members of the community able to use public

transport can reach one within a given time and that alternative transport to a comparable standard is available to people with a physical disability who, because of the current design of most buses, are unable to use scheduled services.

- Equality of treatment – that the same rules and procedures are applied to all who are in a similar situation and that the personal preferences or prejudices of local authority officers or members have no force, for example that housing allocation criteria do not discriminate against certain groups and that personal intervention by elected members does not allow families to jump the queue.
- Equality of use – for example that children of low income families are able to receive the same amount of pre-school education as those whose parents are from higher income groups.
- Equality of outcome – in other words that individuals emerge from the customer process (see Chapter 5) with the same results. In the case of education it might be that the pattern of achievement is the same across all social classes (Le Grand 1983).

Discrimination

In discussions of local authority service delivery discrimination is usually taken to refer to situations where a member of one group is treated less favourably than a member of another, for example by refusing a service to an Asian applicant specifically because of their ethnic origin. Such *direct* discrimination is often the result of personal prejudice on the part of one, or a number of, local authority employees, often reinforced by incorrect and negative stereotypes about the particular group (see Chapter 8). The groups affected may be covered by anti-discrimination legislation but also could be outside its scope (see below). Discrimination on the grounds of age is one example.

There is, however, another form of discrimination. This *indirect* discrimination is usually built into the policies and procedures of the organisation, often remaining hidden from view until monitoring and reviews are undertaken or cases of discrimination brought against the authority. It occurs when a condition or requirement which applies to all:

- has a disproportionate effect on one group;
- is to the detriment of members of that group because they are unable to comply with the condition; and
- is not justifiable on grounds other than the characteristics of the group affected.

In other words, while the authority is treating everyone the same the effects of applying such rules or conditions is to differentially disadvantage a particular group. Local authority housing departments have applied residential requirements which, in certain localities, have been shown to have a disproportionate and detrimental effect on black and ethnic minority applicants. Indirect discrimination is an impediment to local authorities wishing to open up recruitment to groups underrepresented in particular occupations. Fire service selection procedures, for example, have included physical aptitude tests based on male physiques and approaches. As a result women applicants were differentially disadvantaged.

Anti-discrimination legislation

Equality is part of the legal framework within which local authorities operate, although discrimination affects a wider range of groups than are covered by legislation. The Sex Discrimination Act 1975 and the Race Relations Act 1976 prohibit discrimination in employment and the provision of services on the grounds of sex, marital status, race, colour, nationality and ethnic or national origin. The Race Relations Act also places a duty on local authorities to eliminate unlawful discrimination and promote equality of opportunity and good relations between racial groups. These statutes therefore provide clear and explicit criteria which should be adopted in undertaking service reviews, as well as establishing the basis for new policy initiatives.

There are two exceptions to the general requirement not to discriminate, both of which can enhance service quality. The first is where being a man or woman or member of a particular ethnic or national group is an essential requirement for an employee to be able to undertake the job. It would therefore be a *genuine occupational qualification* to appoint a Bangladeshi woman if the post involved outreach work with this group and the authority felt that men or non-Bangladeshi women were unlikely to be able to undertake the task effectively. This statutory provision enables service delivery to be more appropriately tuned to the needs of particular groups. Secondly positive action may be taken where members of groups covered by the legislation are underrepresented in an occupational area. This could involve special training, advertising strategies and other actions designed to ensure that the pool of qualified applicants was more representative. Unlike the United States, however, it is unlawful to discriminate at the point of selection in favour of or against a member of any particular group.

The other main pieces of equality legislation concern conditions of employment rather than service delivery, although these aspects are inter-related (see above). The Disabled Persons (Employment) Act 1944 places a duty on employers with a workforce of more than 20, and where an exemption has not been obtained, to employ at least 3 per cent registered disabled people. This quota is seldom met and additionally disabled people may prefer not to register. The Equal Pay Act 1983 states that women and men carrying out the same work or work of equal value should be paid at the same rate.

Developing quality and equality

The links between quality and equality have begun to be made in a few authorities, but often the two streams of work have been seen as separate. The implications for local authorities wanting to make these connections are twofold. Firstly it is essential to strengthen service quality by taking steps to identify and eliminate any forms of direct discrimination. These may only come to light through complaints, liaison with the local racial equality council or other agencies, independently facilitated qualitative research or consultation. Secondly a methodologically sound form of data collection, analysis and monitoring should be established to enable the indirectly discriminatory effects of uniform treatment to be identified. The fact that everyone is treated the same should not be taken as evidence that discrimination is absent.

The LGMB report identifies specific strategies for interrelating and taking forward quality and equality, some of which are drawn on in chapter 8, and also sets out guidelines for practice (Figure 4.2). It highlights in particular the importance of linking quality and equality in both the authority's work with customers and its internal initiatives with employees.

Figure 4.2: Guidelines for integrating equality and quality

- Recognise the needs specific to each of its customers.
- Ensure that the service package is designed from the perspective of all groups of customers.
- Regularly review its policies and services through the eyes of all groups of customers.
- Design ways of collecting information that reach the whole community.
- Design ways of providing information that are appropriate to its different groups of customers.
- Establish consultation and decision-making processes which enable less-powerful groups to be actively involved.
- Ensure that the composition of staff at all levels reflects that of the community it serves.
- Establish equality and quality as core values for managers and policy-makers.

Source: LGMB 1991

The 3Es – economy, efficiency and effectiveness

The last decade has seen major developments in the theory and practice of performance measurement in the public sector. Among a host of concepts three are particularly important:

- Economy – This refers to the standardised cost of resource inputs, including employees, buildings, equipment and supplies, to any local authority activity. The Audit Commission regards an economical operation as one which 'acquires these resources in the appropriate quantity and quality at the lowest cost' (Audit Commission 1983, para 40).
- Efficiency – This concerns the relationship between the services or other outputs of the local authority's activity and the resources necessary to produce them. An efficient operation results in the maximum output for a given resource input, for example the quickest and most

accurate assessment of housing benefit claims per staff member; or a given level of output for the minimum resource input, for instance attaining the same quality of office cleaning while using a cheaper floor polish.

- Effectiveness – This is a measure of the extent to which the organisation is achieving its objectives. It is an assessment of the relationship betwen the intentions of the authority and the effects or outcomes of its activities.

A simple model of the local authority service process (Figure 4.3) illustrates these concepts.

Figure 4.3: The local authority production process: A model

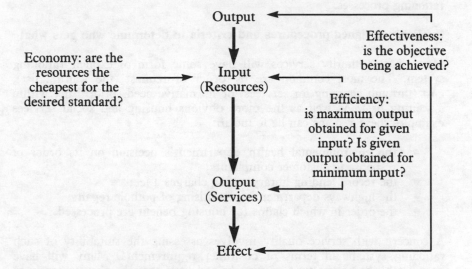

Economy, efficiency and effectiveness should not be ignored when undertaking a service review or redesign. They are an essential part of good management practice. However they are not neutral or objective concepts but must be seen in the context of the authority's political objectives. Exploring economy will raise questions about salary and wage levels, conditions of service and the equipment provided to employees while reviewing efficiency opens up issues about the extent to which facilities or services should be standardised. Different authorities will have different perspectives and values and should therefore search for economy, efficiency and effectiveness in terms of their own political context. For one authority the centralisation of facilities will be the most efficient solution while for another it will be decentralisation and investment in information technology. Those using comparative statistics to assess services must be aware of these and the other factors – different organisational arrangements, accounting conventions and so on – that can explain variations in figures between comparator local authorities. These and other issues relating to performance review are discussed more fully elsewhere (Rogers 1991).

Rationing

Because local authority resources of all kinds are limited their allocation to actual or potential customers is inevitably rationed. Rationing can affect:

- who gains access to a service;
- the order in which customers receive a service;
- the time taken between request and delivery;
- the distance customers have to travel;
- the amount or quality of service a customer obtains.

There are four ways in which rationing takes place, only one of which is deliberately designed to have this effect. Part of the process of reviewing services should therefore be the identification and eradication of unintended rationing processes.

Explicitly designed procedures and criteria to determine who gets what

Many local authority services will have some form of explicit rationing system. The most common are by order of request (the waiting list), cost (through charging for services) or normative need (prioritising within a waiting list). As well as the more obvious housing and social services examples these systems can be found in:

- the environmental health department's decision on its order of response to customer complaints;
- the record lending library which charges a fee;
- the highways department's prioritising of pothole repairs;
- the order in which claims for housing benefit are processed.

A concern with service quality involves assessing the suitability of such rationing systems in terms of customer requirements. Many will have been established some time previously and little thought given recently to their effect or appropriateness. To what extent, for example, do customers understand the system and the criteria applied? Does rationing occur by discouraging applications? New or revised systems, perhaps based on some of the different definions of need and demand discussed above, could be devised.

Customs, traditions and practices which are not designed to, but have, the effect of rationing resources

Some of these were discussed in Chapter 2 – the lack of information to customers, a failure to consider physical access to services and letters written in bureaucratic language. All have the effect of preventing or discouraging some people from making use of services and therefore rationing them. This may have a discriminatory effect, only noticeable when the characteristics of actual customers are matched with those of the whole population for the service. Some of the more common customs, traditions and practices which unintentionally may result in rationing are:

- Office opening between 9.00 am and 5.00 pm Monday to Friday. Where a personal visit is necessary this can cause considerable difficulties and loss of income for customers employed in manual, shop-floor and clerical positions and not able to have the same degree of discretion and autonomy over their working day as many professionals and managers.
- Lack of appointment systems, which result in customers being unaware of their position in a queue and the time they are likely to be seen. These ration by frustration. Someone coming into a waiting area and seeing a mass of people is likely to go away with the intention of returning later. They may or may not do so. Evidence from the health service demonstrates that customers give high priority to the ability to book an appointment and be informed of the reason for any delays which may occur.
- Unwillingness to involve customers in the design of service systems. This causes rationing because those working for the local authority can never fully see things from the customer's perspective. There are always ways in which the service design could be improved.

Because expressed need is often assessed by reference to customer requests for service this form of rationing can result in such statistics under representing the actual situation.

Employees' decisions about the allocation of their time and attention

Because employees only have limited time their decisions about where to devote their energies will result in rationing. In an understaffed and overloaded community charge office the temptation for managers and employees may be to deal with the easier cases which can be processed quickly rather than the more complex ones which will take considerably longer. Professionals also may find certain issues, customer groups and developments more interesting than others and hence allocate their time and skill differentially. An area planning officer's enthusiasm for tree preservation orders can detract from their enforcement responsibilities with the result that one group of customers obtains higher quality service than another. Similarly 'difficult' social work clients or angry parents complaining about a school may be put off as long as possible.

Customers' experiences and perceptions of the local authority

Rationing of services can take place as a result of people's experiences and perceptions of the local authority. Individuals will also gather information about others' experiences of the local authority, especially incidences of poor quality service and situations where the customer felt they were entitled to a service but were not eligible. The resulting feelings of frustration and anger are often expressed to others, stimulating them to recount their personal experiences or similar ones they have heard about (Figure 4.4). Because bad experiences are more noticeable and tend to be recounted more frequently than good ones a collective perception about 'what to expect from the council' can develop in the community. People may therefore decide not to apply for services because

- 'You can never get what you want.'
- 'They always take ages to respond.'
- 'You can wait in ages and they still don't turn up.'
- 'It's never open when you go there.'
- 'They said they'd phone back but they never did.'

Figure 4.4: The development of negative perceptions about the local authority

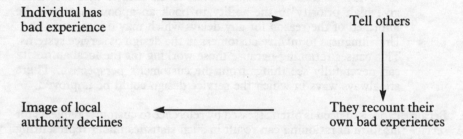

Principles for service choice

Underlying principles are built into local authority decisions, resource allocation and the nature, level and method of service delivery. These often only become explicit when services are reviewed and policy choices are faced. It is therefore important that any redesign of services explicitly identifies the existing and preferred principles and considers their implications for service quality. The main principles are:

- utilitarianism;
- libertarianism;
- redistribution;
- social justice;
- constrained inequality;
- filtering down;
- territorial justice.

Utilitarianism is the concept that public actions should be directed towards the greatest good for the greatest number, in other words that the welfare of most individuals will be increased. This principle is often used in debates about road improvements, for example:

> while constructing a dual carriageway may cause suffering or inconvenience for a few families it will benefit a considerably greater number of road users and businesses as well as relieving conjestion on other routes.

The difficulty in applying this principle is that it is based on a simple majority rule. In the example the many who use road transport benefit at the expense of the few who live on the proposed route. However, given the way the choice is formulated, preference is inevitably given to road users because of their numerical superiority. The principle's simplicity is also its limitation.

Adopting the principle of libertarianism involves reducing the level of local authority provision and regulation on the grounds that people should be free to make their own choices within a minimal governmental framework. It is linked with the argument that in a number of areas of local authority provision the private sector could develop to meet any demand and that the operation of the market will ensure adequate standards. Libertarianist arguments are sometimes heard in discussions of social services policy, for example in relation to residential provision for elderly people. Local authorities applying this principle would need to ensure that the market would respond to the needs it felt should be met and that statutory standards were fulfilled by providers.

The redistributive principle can be expressed in terms of the formulation: to each according to their need, from each according to their ability. Need can be defined in several ways (see above) and ability is often interpreted as wealth. Public provision can therefore be used to redistribute from the wealthier to the poorer or from those with less need to those with more need. One application of this principle is through graduated charging systems in leisure centres where a discount is available to young people, those on low incomes and pensioners.

Social justice states that resources should be distributed in such a way that the least advantaged members of society are not made worse off. For example:

- the local authority would protect provision to the most disadvantaged groups when determining service reductions; or
- it might build a new sports facility in an affluent locality but not at the cost of reducing similar provision in poorer areas.

In other words wealthier, employed or otherwise advantaged groups could gain greater benefits from the local authority as long as provision for the disadvantaged remained constant in real terms. The application of this principle, however, could result in a greater disparity between areas and groups of customers. It also takes as given the existing level of provision for poorer areas or groups without asking whether this is adequate.

Constrained inequality provides an alternative to the principle of social justice. Here the local authority would accept the existence of service inequalities but only within specified limits. For example in a rural area the local education authority might plan primary school provision so that the furthest a child had to travel was five miles.

Under the principle of filtering down the local authority would distribute resources towards centres of economic, social or cultural success in the belief that the benefits of such investment would filter down to less advantaged or successful groups. For example:

by instigating promotional strategies and offering low cost industrial sites and workforce training local authorities attempt to attract business concerns in the hope that their expenditure on employees, goods and services will have a beneficial effect on the local economy.

However it is important to establish the extent to which the system (in this case the local economy) is closed. In other words will the business import trained workers from elsewhere and purchase few supplies from the locality? In this case the benefits which filter down may be few when set against the investment by the local authority. This principle is also applied within the local authority when additional finance is allocated to centres of excellence such as service outlets who achieve a high level of performance. The assumption is that this will have a filtering down effect by encouraging others to attain improvements in their standards (see Chapter 7).

Territorial justice involves the local authority distributing resources between localities in a manner that corresponds with the varying needs of those areas. It rests on the assumption that different localities have different needs and that these are not reflected in the existing pattern of resource allocation – either as a deliberate result of public policy (such as the filtering down principle discussed above) or because of wider political processes. In the health services, for example, it has been suggested that there is an inverse care law. This law, which in fact is a hypothesis since the evidence to support it is ambiguous, states that the spatial availability of good medical care tends to vary inversely with the need of the population (Powell 1990).

These principles contain substantially different interpretations of what is or is not a fair distribution of public resources and services. Some will argue that it is most just to concentrate resources on centres of excellence, rewarding the successful and stimulating the filtering down of benefits; others will make the case that this process is unproven and therefore that the local authority should actively redistribute from higher to lower income groups. Part of the purpose of service review is to identify the principle on which past provision has been determined, to assess its appropriateness and to offer alternatives. To decide the future pattern involves professional advice and investigation, but ultimately is a political choice. It will reflect local political values and priorities and the weight elected members give to the views of citizens, customers and officers.

Applying the concepts in practice

The concepts discussed in this chapter underlie the decisions and practices of local authorities in designing and delivering services and inform the policy context within which this activity takes place. Improving service quality inevitably raises questions of the needs of different groups, the equality of service provision and the level of economy, efficiency and effectiveness. Being clear what these and the other concepts mean and how they can be applied in practice is therefore essential for managers and elected members.

5 Designing the service relationship

The provision and use of services involves a relationship between the customer and the local authority. This can take different forms. It may be direct and personal such as that between adult literacy teacher and student or formal and imposed, for example prosecuting a restaurant owner. In other services the relationship will be indirect and impersonal, as between a driver and the highways department. The explicit design of the service relationship is essential in order to achieve service quality. Leaving the relationship to chance or past practice is no guarantee that it will be satisfactory and almost certainly reviewing it from the customer's perspective will result in improvements.

Designing the service relationship involves a number of elements, each of which is discussed in more detail in this chapter:

- specifying the service package – being clear what is to be provided, when, how and to whom;
- the design of the customer process – setting out the way in which people will receive, gain access to or use the service;
- the role of customer-contact employees – and their particular significance in the relationship between customer and local authority;
- service guarantees – being clear with customers what the service package consists of and ensuring its delivery;
- complaints systems – detailing ways in which customers can raise issues with the local authority.

The level of service quality will be determined as much by the process through which each element is designed as the final result. Not only is the involvement of all parties likely to lead to a better form of service relationship being established, but the act of consultation, liaison, negotiation and participation will demonstrate the authority's commitment to building a better relationship with customers and to improving service quality.

Specifying the service package

The service package consists of the set of activities, interactions and resources through which the customer and local authority interrelate, and its specification is becoming an increasingly common part of local authority practice as a result of CCT and other changes. The specification of the service package requires information on:

- the views of actual and potential customers;
- changes in the demographic, social, economic and physical environment of the area;
- the political values and priorities of elected members;
- financial, human and physical resources;
- legal requirements and conditions;
- best practice advice from service delivery staff, managers and professionals;
- information from other local authorities, outside agencies and interested parties.

The methods used to obtain such information might include those discussed in Chapters 3 and 4.

In the past the design of service packages was frequently partial and incremental and the customer's perspective was often marginalised or ignored. Service frequency or methods of provision might be reviewed and changed at one moment while the physical environment for the service (for example, reception areas) only came under scrutiny at a later date. Often customers were not consulted about their requirements. The service specification was seldom clearly and comprehensively codified. Authorities might provide brief leaflets for customers and issue employees with procedure guides, but frequently the documentation was limited and incomplete.

As part of the move to improve service quality there is now widespread interest in developing clear specifications of the service package and publicising this to customers. This takes a number of forms depending on the particular relationships involved (Figure 5.1):

- Between client and contractor – this involves the *service specification* describing the work to be done and the contract conditions which detail the relationship between the parties.
- Between service delivery and support functions within the local authority – these *service level agreements* form an explicit internal agreement about the support services to be provided (financial data, industrial relations advice, legal advice) and the charging rate.
- Between local authority and customers – service guarantees (also termed customer contracts, service promises or public service agreements) provide customers with information on the service to be provided and a clear procedure in the event of service failure (see below).

Designing the customer process

Taking a customer-centred approach to specifying the service package should involve the local authority in reviewing and explicitly designing the process through which customers come into contact with the organisation and its activities. A framework which illustrates this service system is presented

Figure 5.1: Service relationships and contract forms

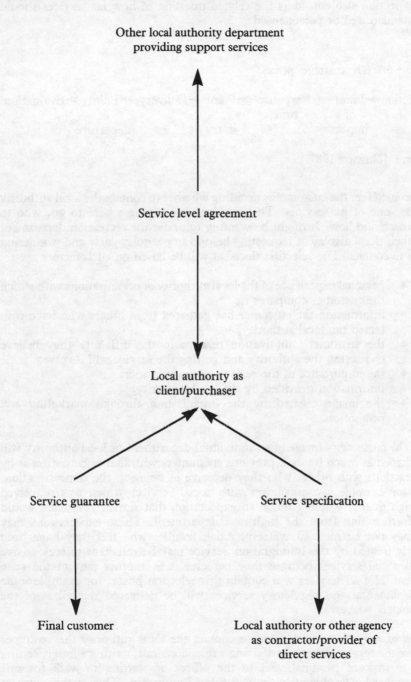

Other local authority department
providing support services

Service level agreement

Local authority as
client/purchaser

Service guarantee   Service specification

Final customer   Local authority or other agency
as contractor/provider of
direct services

in Figure 5.2. It comprises four stages linked by a number of key points. This section also considers the related question of how far services should be standardised or personalised.

Figure 5.2: The customer process

Selection➤Point➤ Response ➤Point➤Delivery➤Point ➤Evaluation
                 of   time   of   of
             impact   entry   departure

Source: Johnston 1987

Selection: Here the customer is deciding whether to contact the local authority or use one of its services. This involves identifying where to go, who to approach and how. It might be wanting to praise the recreation department for their floral display or requesting help to stop a noisy party and wondering who to contact. The selection decision will be based on such factors as:

- personal experience of the local authority or organisations with which the customer compares it;
- information the customer has gathered from others who have contacted the local authority;
- the customer's motivation relative to the difficulty they believe contacting the authority and getting the service will involve;
- the importance of the service to the customer;
- information provided by the local authority;
- the image created by the organisation through marketing and promotion.

The customer's image of an individual department or local authority will be shaped as much by their previous encounters with that organisation as by interactions with others who they perceive as being in the same situation. So, for example, an encounter with social services which was perceived as high quality would tend to an expectation that similar responses would be forthcoming from the highways department. These expectations may or may not be met. Conversely, Asian families who feel they have been poorly treated by the Immigration Service may be reluctant to seek advice from social services because they perceive it as another part of the state system. Not all services will contain this selection phase, for example some environmental and regulatory services will be delivered regardless of the customers wishes.

Point of entry: Having decided to contact the local authority the customer enters the service system by starting a telephone call, writing a letter, setting out to make a personal visit to the offices or starting to walk towards someone who is obviously from the local authority. This is the point at which customers tend to make their first, and often lasting, evaluation of service quality:

The development of perceptions about the quality of service begins at the point of entry . . . For a first-time entrant to a service organisation this can be a most unnerving time as the customer searches for clues as to what to do and how to behave (Johnston 1987, p.42).

Factors such as ease of access, clear and visible information on procedures and signposting will affect the customer's perception of service quality.

Response time: On entering the service system the customer will have to wait for someone to attend to them, identify their needs and take appropriate action. This will involve queueing. The queue may be of other customers at a reception desk or on a waiting list; alternatively it could be a queue of priorities – the employee dealing with other matters (including other employees) before responding to the customer. The perceived response time will influence the customer's evaluation of service quality. Because perceived waiting time is affected by the service surroundings some organisations have improved the reception area in an attempt to reduce the customer's sense of delay. This may be appropriate, for instance if an interview in a neighbourhood office overruns, but in other cases it may be just an attempt to disguise a poorly designed service package.

Point of impact: This is the moment when an employee acknowledges and responds to the customer and the process of service delivery begins. This can be a critical moment for the customer and the employee. The customer may expect the employee to be able to solve their problem or at least show an adequate level of competence, skill and understanding. They may also perceive the employee as representing and being knowledgeable about the whole organisation and able to provide access to other areas of service. In this respect the customer will often be disappointed.

Delivery: The delivery system is activated by customer contact employees. It may involve a set of organisational routines – allocating housing points, evaluating a grant application from a voluntary group, following-up an environmental health complaint – through which decisions are made and the services requested are offered, denied or alternatives presented. Alternatively it may take place through personal interaction as in the case of an adult education class. The customer will again assess service quality at this point.

Point of departure: When service delivery is complete the customer leaves the service system. For some local authority services the sequence from selection to departure may take a relatively short time – requesting volumes from the County Records Office – while in the case of compulsory education it will occur over a decade or more. In certain instances departure may occur because of the failure of the local authority to deliver services effectively or appropriately, for instance by wrongly diagnosing the customer's needs at the point of impact. Alternatively the customer may opt to leave the service system despite still needing the facilities provided. This might occur because:

- customers exercise their right to take over the authority's assets, for example by purchasing a council house; or
- the service is not delivered in an appropriate way, for example an elderly person withdrawing from the home help service because their worker is changed without consultation.

Some groups of customers, such as children in care, remain tied to the delivery system without the choice of exit.

Evaluation: Once the customer has left the service system they will evaluate their experience. This can be a conscious or subconscious process. It may have no noticeable effect or it may lead to letters of praise or complaint. It can also result in conversations with other members of the community and hence affect actual or potential customers' perception of the authority's service quality. In this way it feeds back into the start of the process – the selection decision.

The reality of the customer process will often be more complex than this. There may be sequential or parallel service or delivery systems, for example requesting a book held at another branch library will involve staff at the customer's library themselves accessing a service system. The employees the customer comes into contact with will therefore be limited in what they are able to offer by the operation of another service system. In this way all activities of the local authority ultimately affect the external customer (see Chapter 8).

Standardisation and personalisation: Local authorities concerned with service quality face a dilemma. On the one hand customers want to be treated as individuals and receive a service package that closely meets their requirements. On the other they desire an efficient and equitable service and want to be treated fairly. And overlaying this tension is the need for rules and controls in a large publicly accountable bureaucracy. The issue for service quality is where to establish the balance between standardisation and personalisation.

One approach is to soften the bluntness of standardisation by ensuring customer contact staff have good personal skills. In some services this may be desirable from the organisation's as well as the customer's perspective. For example, the ability of housing benefit staff to relate to the customer as an individual enables applicants to feel relaxed and hence makes it easier to gather the complex, sensitive and personal information required. Because the subsequent calculation of benefit is largely administrative it can be standardised without detriment to the customer – provided all possible cases are covered by the rules and there is an appeal mechanism. The service might be further personalised through home visits by officers and translation of letters and other information into the applicant's mother tongue where this is not English.

Because local authorities are bureaucracies, they have tended to place personalisation second to standardisation. Standardisation enables managerial control to be exercised more effectively than in a personalised service and is more appropriate to the forms of upward accountability which currently predominate. The question for local authorities developing service quality is: what is the minimum level of standardisation necessary? Designing a service system from the customer's perspective implies that personalisation should come first.

Developing the front-line of service delivery

Customer contact employees operate as gatekeepers managing the relationship between the customer and the local authority. This can involve a number of activities:

- Defining or redefining the customer's requirements in terms of what the local authority has to offer. Customer contact staff attempt to match the customer to the organisation's range of available responses, for example when a receptionist interprets a customer's problem in terms of the departments and sections of the authority.
- Controlling access to the local authority and its services by ensuring that customers meet certain eligibility criteria. These criteria might include payment, length of residence, age, income and having correctly completed a form.
- Determining the local authority response. Because of their location at the boundary of the organisation customer contact staff have a degree of discretion in determining how the local authority will respond. This discretion is relatively limited for clerical and reception staff operating within bureaucratic structures, but is more extensive for professionals.

For many customers these employees who have the most significant effect on *perceived* service quality. In a study of the way in which DSS claimants evaluated service quality, helpful and knowledgeable staff were the two most frequently mentioned factors. For local authority tenants it was staff who explained and staff who understood (Figure 5.3). The personal behaviour and skill of individuals in customer contact roles is therefore particularly important from the customer's perspective, not least because local authority services often involve considerable interaction between customer and employee. The design of the service process should therefore give explicit consideration to the role, skills and expected behaviour of employees at the point of customer contact.

The interactions between customers and local authority employees take many different forms (Figure 5.4). The examples in Figure 5.4 illustrate the issues that local authorities should address when designing the service relationship.

The customer is the only party to experience the complete service relationship with the local authority. In example 1 the environmental health officer has no understanding of the customer's earlier conversations with the telephonist or housing receptionist. From the viewpoint of the local authority employees involved, each contact with the customer was discreet and with each action they were trying to be helpful. Unfortunately for the customer this process of successive approximations was a less than satisfactory experience.

Figure 5.3: Employee attributes valued by customers

Survey of local authority tenants	% citing as important
Staff who understand problem	50
Staff who explain things	46
Friendly staff	24

Survey of DSS claimants	
Staff who are helpful	82
Staff who seem knowledgeable	79
Staff who have time for me	78
Staff who are polite	74
Staff who are friendly	66

Source: Walsh 1990; National Audit Office 1988

In practice service quality is only partly determined by the customer contact employee. The customer's perception that the employee is the most important factor results from a belief that the individual has more power than may actually be the case. For the customer the employee *is* the organisation and is able to determine its response to the particular situation. What the

Figure 5.4: Examples of interactions between customers and the local authority

Example 1: The wall
'Hello, Borough Council. Can I help you?'
'Is that the Council? There's an empty house next door and the garden wall's fallen on the street.'
'I'll put you through to the housing department. They should be able to help you. Hold on.'
'Hello! Housing.'
'Hello? There's an empty house next door and the garden wall's fallen on the street.'
'Is it a council house?'
'I don't know. It's been empty a long time and I've only recently moved in here.'
'What's the address?'
'49 Lower Street.'
'Doesn't sound like one of ours. I'll have to transfer you to environmental health. They deal with health hazards.'
'But could you take the details . . . hello? hello? Are you there?'
'Jameson, private sector.'
'Hello? Is that the council?'
'Yes, Jameson, private sector housing.'
'Oh (*bemused*). Well (*cautiously*), there's an empty house next door and the garden wall's fallen on the street.'
'Do you know who owns the house?'
'Of course I don't (*getting short tempered*). Look, my 10p's nearly run out and I haven't got any change.'
'Well, it's probably a job for cleansing (*getting annoyed in response to the customer's irritation*). But what's the address?'
'49 Low . . . (*runs out of money and is cut off*).

Example 2: The swimming pool
'Gimme a ticket for a swim, luv!'
'That's 75p, please.'
'I ain't got it. I'll just go for a swim and bring the money in tomorrow.'
(Cashier smells alcohol on customer's breath) 'I'm sorry, sir, but you have to pay
before you go in.' *(There is no panic button so she looks round for a recreation
assistant to help deal with the situation. She cannot see one.)*
'All I want is a **** swim' *(getting aggressive)*.
(Cashier notes queue building up) 'If you'll just wait over there for a minute I'll
see if we can sort it out.'
'Yeah, that's **** right. Get the boss. I know him. He'll tell you to let me in.
You're all the **** same. Get a bit of **** authority and you think you can
treat me like this!' *(starting to shout, other customers backing away)*.
*(At last a recreation assistant comes in sight. Cashier calls her over to deal with the
drunk customer so that she can get on with letting other people into the pool.)*

Example 3: The restaurant inspection
'Having inspected the food preparation arrangements I've noted a number of
ways in which you fail to meet the statutory standards. There are what appear
to be rodent droppings beside the storage cupboard and the refrigeration
arrangements are not adequate or working satisfactorily. I've also noticed that
the staff washing and toilet facilities are unhygienic.'
'Oh, but my customers are happy. *(Goes out into eating area and asks customers.)*
You're happy with the food I provide aren't you? You've no complaints? *(Nods
of agreement from customers.)* You see, there is no problem. No-one is ill.'
'I'm sorry, sir, but these regulations are designed to make sure that no-one
ever becomes ill. You'll have to improve your standards. What we need to do
is decide on the course of action. I could instigate legal proceedings with the
evidence I have collected, but in this instance I feel that a warning would be
appropriate. I'll come on a return inspection next week and expect to see the
faults rectified. If they are not, then I'll have no option but to recommend
prosecution. Do you understand?'
'Yes, yes. Thank you. I'll certainly clean the place up. And you'd be welcome
as my guest any time. Please bring your wife and family too! I will personally
cook you my special dishes!'

customer will often be unaware of are the sets of rules and procedures which
shape the employee's actions. Employees work in a bureaucratic context of
which the customer is only dimly aware. However polite, understanding and
sympathetic they may not be able to deliver what the customer wants. In
example 3 legal action will follow if the inspector returns to find the faults
not rectified – whatever the restaurant owner or his customers want.

Organisational factors can constrain employees from taking a course of
action which would lead to the customer experiencing good service quality.
It is common to hear managers complain that they have employees with a
'jobsworth' attitude to customers – as in 'I can't do that, it's more than my
job's worth.' This discounts the power relationships within which employees
work and the absence of a culture and reward system which would encourage

wider definitions of their role. In example 1 the housing receptionist has little inclination to take the details of the collapsed wall and pass them on to the correct person because she has just been told to photocopy a set of reports urgently for an assistant director. Because managers in the department only have a partial and limited understanding of what happens to customers who phone in, the telephonist has not received instructions on how to respond and whether to give such customers more priority than a manager.

Customers are not always polite and reasonable. Some customers can be rude, aggressive, racist and violent as in example 2. This is more likely in certain services than others. Being on the counter in a city housing office can involve heated exchanges sparked by the frustration and desperation of homeless people and those living in overcrowded or sub-standard accommodation. Customer contact staff have to absorb these emotions while responding as best they can to the requests being made of them. They can feel trapped between the demands of customers and the lack of resources with which to meet them. They can find themselves covering vacant or frozen posts and for colleagues who are on sick leave as a result of the stresses they are placed under. This organisational context does not contribute to service quality.

Redesigning the customer contact role

It is important to understand the context within which customer contact employees operate when developing initiatives to improve service quality. Some local authority managers share the customer's view and perceive the behaviour of customer contact employees as the key determinant of service quality. This can lead to skill training sessions and pep talks on politeness which, while an important element, should not be seen in isolation from the wider organisational context within which the employee operates.

The key criteria for redesigning the customer contact role are:

- Deal with as many customer requests as possible at the first point of contact. Customer contact staff should be trained and resourced to operate in a generic role for as wide a range of functions as possible. While for certain areas it will be necessary to involve specialists, the expectation should be that routine requests across the organisation's activities are dealt with at the first point of contact. This will involve . . .
- . . . Redefining the role of receptionists and telephonists from customer redirection to problem solving. The authority should accept that the customer contact employee's role is to ensure that the organisation responds to customer requests within its policy framework, and to highlight areas where this seems inadequate. It will require changing the job descriptions, grading and skills of these employees, and . . . .
- . . . Improving the relationship between those in customer contact roles and the rest of the organisation. Quality of service to customers by the 'front-line' is affected by the quality of service they themselves receive from the 'back-line' – those in specialist and support roles.

- Take advantage of information technology to enable a greater number of single point customer contacts. Computer systems can enable direct customer access to information as well as provide employees with a larger information base from which to respond to customers.
- Design an effective support system for those in customer contact positions. Delivering service direct to customers can be a difficult and demanding job, and operating in a generic and advocacy role the more so. It requires effective support – in human, financial, physical and political terms.

Local authorities have responded to these issues in different ways:

- Solihull MBC has developed a programe of customer care courses. An initial workshop is provided for all employees having contact with customers. It includes an introduction to customer service action groups within which employees can develop proposals to improve service quality. Members of these groups have direct access to the deputies group who hold a small budget to fund quality innovations. More specific courses are also offered, including 'dealing with customers with a hearing loss' and 'handling aggressive situations'. In 1989 Solihull received a National Training Award for its 'customer first' training programme.
- A number of local authorities, including Bury MBC and Coventry City Council, have worked with receptionists to redesign their role. Some authorities have regraded these posts and invested in training, increasing the status of employees and their ability to play a greater part in resolving customer enquiries and requests. In some cases receptionists have become uniformed. These changes are often part of a corporate strategy to improve reception areas and access to council offices, including redesigned layout and new telephone systems.
- New technology is being used by several authorities to give customers greater access to information. Birmingham City Council has a database which can be accessed by customers through terminals in libraries and neighbourhood offices, and the possibility of placing them in non-local authority locations is also being investigated.
- Islington and Wrekin are amongst the authorities encouraging senior managers to spend time with customer contact employees as a normal part of their managerial role. This *service sampling* is designed to provide managers with a better understanding of the point of service delivery and the issues faced both by customers and employees.

Service guarantees

Service guarantees (also referred to as public service agreements and customer contracts) have been developed in several local authorities and other public and recently privatised agencies. They are a method of being clear with customers what service is being provided, to what standard and of specifying their rights and power (Figure 5.5).

Figure 5.5: Contents of a service guarantee

1. Statement of services to be provided:
    - what the service is
    - how it is provided
    - who it serves
    - where it is available
    - what frequency or other standards it will meet
    - criteria for access to the service
    - behaviour expected of staff or the authority's agents
    - behaviour expected of customers
    - what it costs customers
2. Rights of the customer in using the service:
    - the right to be able to choose within the service
    - the right not to be discriminated against by virtue of gender, ethnic origin, location, disability, etc.
    - the right to have any specific needs met
    - the right to be consulted about the service specification and have the opportunity to contribute to its review
3. Contact point for customers – the named individual responsible for managing the service, office address and phone number and hotlines available for 24 hour cover
4. Procedure in the event of service failure or variation – what the authority undertakes to do in the event of the service not being available or not meeting the specified standard, including alternative provision and time targets to restore service
5. Rights of customers in the event of service failure – this might include access to alternative provider or service, compensation arrangements, complaints procedure and independent arbiter.

Some service guarantees, for example on street lighting or refuse collection, will be relatively straightforward to develop because of the discrete nature of the service activity. Others, particularly in social services and education, will be more complex and may differ from customer to customer (Figure 5.6). The specification of standards is also not always simple. It is clear when a bin has not been collected but what is clean water in a swimming pool? Islington LB consulted with users and adopted their definition: pool water is clean if the bottom of the pool is clearly visible at all times and there is no floating debris.

Figure 5.6: Services – Some dimensions

		Nature of Service	
		Discrete	*Open-ended*
	Individual	Refuse collection	Adult literacy
		Home help	Trading standards
Focus			
	Group	Street sweeping	Community
		Parks	development

The experience of service guarantees

Some examples of authorities who have introduced service guarantees are:

- York – street cleansing and refuse collection: Service guarantees were part of a series of corporate initiatives designed to improve service quality. They were piloted in two neighbourhoods with active residents' associations. The 'easy' services of refuse collection and street cleansing were chosen, and from the CCT specification a service guarantee was developed. This was distributed to all households in the area and contained a description of which streets would be swept or have refuse collected and when, the method, standard and cost of cleansing and a hot-line phone number to call if there was a complaint. A clear procedure for dealing with complaints was devised.
- Islington – meals on wheels: Islington had already implemented a quality programme, including service guarantees for some environmental services. The customer contract for meals on wheels was developed through a quality audit involving discussions with customers and providers. It involved a review of the service from the customer's perspective leading to significant changes in the method of delivery.
- Solihull – library services: Customers are provided with a book marker which gives details of service standards the department seeks to achieve in responding to reference enquiries, book requests and other issues. It also undertakes to conduct a customer satisfaction survey annually and publish the results.
- Harlow – core guarantees: Harlow Council has introduced a set of principles which apply to all services (Figure 5.7). In addition service promises for individual outlets are being drawn up and will be prominently displayed at the relevant facility or in other ways.

Figure 5.7: Harlow Council's core guarantees

- Courteous, polite and helpful staff at all public points of service delivery
- Telephone answered promptly, with names given and no 'holding on'
- All letters acknowledged within five working days
- All Council front-line facilities to be welcoming, attractive and user-friendly
- Every effort made to keep appointments and to fit in with domestic arrangements
- Senior managers to be accessible to service users

Source: Harlow DC

The experience with service guarantees to date highlights three main lessons. Firstly service performance tends to improve. This is partly because employees now know what is expected of them and are better able to perceive a customer for their services. The creation of a clear job specification and quality standards removes much of the ambiguity and discretion which in the past has contributed to poor service quality. Additionally, however, service guarantees give employees a clearer sense of ownership of the service and they have a stronger basis for making claims on the organisation for the equipment and training necessary to achieve and maintain standards. Secondly the guarantee must be achieveable. Service guarantees change the authority's relationship with customers and increase the organisation's accountability. The publication of service costs in the guarantee, as Rochdale MBC do for refuse collection, is therefore important. The inclusion of a sanction, albeit a token one, may strengthen this accountability link. Finally service guarantees to be effective must be related to other initiatives. Employees and customers should be fully involved with managers and elected members in reviewing and redesigning the service. Training of employees is important, as is the development of managers able to operate in this new form of relationship with customers. Because an individual customer has a number of relationships with the local authority there may be pressure for guarantees in other services.

Figure 5.8: Advantages and disadvantages of service guarantees

Advantages	**Disadvantages**
Clear criteria for service eligibility	Used as rationing mechanism in time of cut-back
Public awareness of service and authority's role	Is it a maximum or minimum standard?
Reduces misunderstandings and false expectations	Inflexible if needs change
Improves service quality	Is there a budget to finance necessary variations?
Increases employee commitment and performance	
Enforces awareness of resources needed to achieve the specification	

There are, however, difficulties in adopting service guarantees (Figure 5.8). The promise of explicit service standards may be used to conceal real reductions in resources or provide a gloss on stricter rationing criteria. Developing a specification could remove discretion essential to the provision of service to a changing customer group or where new needs appear. The failure to consult with customers could result in a well prepared but inappropriate service. Finally, the standards specified might be treated as the maximum and the budget constructed on this basis allowing little flexibility if conditions change. In some services the guarantee might more appropriately be set as the minimum. For example, the minimum meals on wheels service might be one hot meal a day, but in extreme cold weather this could be increased to two for some customers.

Key issues in designing service guarantees

Deciding whether to develop a service guarantee. Service guarantees should not be adopted lightly. They are an important statement by the local authority about its relationship with customers and employees. They are not a quick fix to improve the authority's image but are part of becoming more service quality focussed. They will require time, energy, commitment and finance.

Deciding in which service to develop a service guarantee. It is easier to develop service guarantees in some services than others. Political considerations or the results of market research may determine that one service is given priority. If the service guarantee is publicised to every household, remember that it must compete with other advertising literature for the customer's attention.

(Re)designing the service. This involves establishing the service specification through a process of identifying what customers, employees, elected members and others think of the current service (if there is one) and identifying preferred changes. Because service guarantees are about a more open relationship between customers and the local authority this should be mirrored in the service redesign process. Appropriate forms of market research and consultation should be used, for example customer surveys and forums, quality audits and service sampling (see Chapter 3). Because of their experience and knowledge employees should be fully involved in this process.

Establishing customer information and response systems. A service guarantee should contain an effective system by which customers can inform the authority of any shortfall in service provision or changes in their circumstances. Only part of this would therefore be a complaints system. Attention should be paid to designing a customer-friendly system and to ensuring that the authority is able to respond to the information it receives. It is important that the individual at the end of a telephone hot-line has the status and authority to ensure that speedy and appropriate action is taken.

Alternative provision and financial compensation. Some public and recently privatised agencies pay financial compensation if service levels are not met. For example, Severn Trent Water plc provide £5 compensation if:

- staff fail to keep an appointment;
- a reply to a billing enquiry is not received within 20 working days;
- a reply to a complaint about water and sewerage services is not received within 10 days;
- after a notified interruption to service, supplies are not restored; £5 is also payable for each additional day the customer is without supplies.

Similarly, British Rail have introduced a financial compensation scheme which provides travel vouchers to customers who complain because their train is significantly delayed.

Where services are delivered to specific individuals or groups the failure to meet the specification could be compensated through alternative provision, for example a free return visit to a leisure centre or the use of a private builder for local authority housing repairs. Financial compensation is another method, more applicable where alternative provision is not possible. Lewisham LB has undertaken:

- to refund a householder £1 (equivalent to two weeks' refuse collection costs) if three conditions are met:
    - the refuse container is placed on the edge of the property by 7 am on the day of collection;
    - the refuse is not collected and a phone call to report this is made before 6 pm that evening; and
    - the refuse is still not collected the same day.
- to provide a £10 gift voucher to any environmental services customer who makes a written complaint and does not receive a reply within ten working days.

There are several key issues for the local authority contemplating financial compensation. First it must clearly define those situations in which the customer has the right to access the alternative provider or qualify for compensation. This is important both for customers and those employees expected to operate the system. Secondly it should consider the level of financial resources necessary to fund compensation claims by customers as a result of the authority's failure to meet the specification and the impact of this on the budget, especially where this is ring-fenced. Thirdly and most importantly the local authority should establish the purpose of financial compensation. Is it:

- to penalise the service?
- to be a token of goodwill to the customer?
- to sharpen the focus of managers and employees?

They raise the question of who is being penalised. Paying compensation from already tight budgets could ultimately penalise the customers who the authority is trying to serve. One approach to designing redress methods is, as several authorities have done, to ask the customers themselves. In this way the compensation arrangements can be made appropriate to customers' requirements and expectations.

Monitoring the guarantee. The service guarantee is not a once-and-for-all affair. The local authority should use complaints, user panels and other devices to monitor the service and take steps to redesign it when necessary.

Local authorities already have a range of service agreements with customers. For example replacing a street light bulb when it fails, the tenancy agreement, responding to an insect infestation problem, reserving a library book. In a few local authority services, legislation provides for standard specification and compensation, for example the recent Environmental Protection Act in relation to street cleansing. A number of these also place implicit or explicit obligations on the customer – for example to pay their rent. The significance of the customer contract is that it is an explicit

statement of the rights and obligations of both parties and requires the local
authority to think about the wider issues of service quality – timing, access,
standards, equity, courtesy and so on.

Complaints

The final element in the service relationship is the complaints process.
Complaints can be of many different forms:

- disagreement with a policy or procedure;
- the service not being provided as specified;
- a general dissatisfaction with the local authority;
- an action by someone else, for example a street trader, that the
  customer thinks the local authority should deal with;
- the way the individual has been treated by officers or members;
- maladministration;
- the individual not being eligible for, or the authority not providing,
  the service the individual wants;
- the actions of another public sector or recently privatised agency
  which the individual thinks is part of the local authority;
- not being able to find the right person to talk to.

Some complaints the local authority will want to encourage. For the
trading standards, environmental health and planning enforcement functions
to work effectively public complaints are essential. The public in these cases
are acting as unpaid inspectors, notifying the authority of situations where
they believe it should exercise its regulatory powers. Complaints also provide
a means of monitoring service quality from the customer's perspective – the
street light not working, the refuse sack not collected, the difficulty of
getting a pram into a library and the meal-on-wheels delivered cold. Some
complaints will be justified and reflect a failure on the part of the local
authority; others may be malicious or based on incorrect information or
a strongly held anti-local authority view. Some will be minor and others
serious.

Making complaints

Complaints arrive in different ways. Sometimes it will be a formal written
complaint copied to the MP; at other times it will be a passing comment to
a gardener or library assistant – perhaps about something unrelated to their
own service. Because of the perceived power of the local authority some
groups may be unwilling to complain or point out aspects of service delivery
which they find unsatisfactory. Yet inviting, monitoring and responding to
comments and complaints is necessary if service quality is to be improved.
Research for the Widdicombe Committee (Widdicombe 1986) explored
people's attitudes to and experience of complaining to the local authority.
In a national survey conducted by NOP Market Research Ltd. almost half
the respondants said that they had wanted to complain about 'something
the (local) council has done or failed to do'. The three most frequently

mentioned areas for complaint were roads/traffic/parking (23 per cent), council housing/rents (21 per cent) and street cleansing/refuse (15 per cent). However only just over half these respondants actually went on to make a complaint. The two main reasons were:

- 'there was no point/nothing would be done/they would not listen'; and
- 'never got around to it/no time/couldn't be bothered/too lazy'.

That less than half of those with a complaint went on to express it to the local authority has important implications for the design of complaints systems (see below). This picture is reflected in a more recent study which also revealed a disinclination by customers to complain or take further action where they were dissatisfied with the outcome of their contact with the local authority (Figure 5.9).

Figure 5.9: Customer's dissatisfaction and intention to take further action

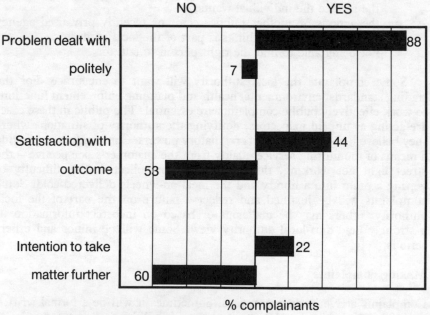

% complainants

Source: Walsh and Davis 1991

Local authorities' approach to complaints

Even where people do decide to make a complaint a recent study has demonstrated that local authorities frequently do not make the process easy or use the information they obtain to improve service quality:

- While almost half of local authorities claimed to have a complaints procedure in many this amounted to little more than a suggestion

that individuals pursue their complaint up the bureaucratic hierarchy.
- Formalised complaints procedures were most frequently found in social services departments and least frequently in education.
- Few local authorities publicise their complaints procedures to citizens and customers.
- Complaints procedures were most frequently a means of allocating staff responsibility rather than enabling complainants to make their voices heard.
- Few departments or authorities log, analyse or monitor complaints.
- Few departments or authorities use complaints as an element in the review process (Seneviratne and Cracknell 1988).

Recently, however, local authorities have become more interested in formal complaints systems. Social services and education departments have a statutory duty to establish them in particular functions and in services subject to CCT complaints are now a key indicator of contractor performance. A variety of methods and formalised systems are now being developed:

- In Harlow DC the chief executive can be contacted directly on the main town hall reception desk for two hours every Friday morning. His support staff will contact the appropriate department and provide a quick answer to any matters of concern or complaints. Complainants are later contacted by phone to ensure they are satisfied with the outcome and the treatment they received.
- Islington has a central complaints unit in the chief executive's department which monitors complaints and identifies patterns requiring investigation.
- Barrow BC conducts exit polls asking about such matters as waiting time, treatment and provision of information. The freepost postcard also invites ideas about ways of improving service and offers in return a voucher which can be used towards refreshments or tickets at the authority's arts centre.
- Stirling DC has produced two simply designed postcards, one for comments and the other for complaints. The aim is to gather suggestions and ideas from customers as well as provide an easy way of making more serious complaints.

Complaints and the Ombudsman

The Commission for Local Administration (CLA) is the main focus for complaints if they are not satisfactorily resolved by the local authority. Individuals are now able to make a complaint directly to the CLA if they have first given the local authority the opportunity to investigate it. Previously complaints could only be referred through the councillor. The CLA's remit is constrained to injustice arising from maladministration – complaints relating to policy questions are not considered. There has been a steadily rising trend of complaints to the CLA particularly concerning social services. Of the 7000 complaints made in 1989–90 81 per cent were discontinued after considering the authority's response or because at a later stage it became clear there had been no maladministration, 15 per cent were subsequently settled locally and only 4 per cent led to a report.

In earlier years the CLA had expressed concern about the failure of some local authorities to provide remedies for injustice caused where maladministration had been found. The final formal action open to the CLA is to issue a further report. Between 1981 and 1990 these were issued in 136 (8 per cent) of maladministration cases. However only 33 satisfactory settlements have been achieved and in another 97 cases the authority concerned has refused to provide a satisfactory remedy. The Local Government and Housing Act 1989 introduced a range of measures designed to improve the procedures by which maladministration reports are considered, but the ultimate decision on whether or not to provide a remedy for injustice remains with the local authority. However much the authority disagrees with the CLA's findings the principles of service quality are not served by a failure to accept the results of an independent investigation.

- A number of local authorities have now decided as a matter of policy to accept the results of any CLA report and provide a satisfactory remedy.
- Buckinghamshire CC, Harlow DC and Lambeth LB have appointed their own internal Ombudspersons to investigate complaints made by members of the public and draw lessons for improving service quality.

There are other routes for complaints, for example the District Auditor or through the legal system. While often of significance in interpreting statute they form a relatively small proportion of complaints.

Designing effective complaints systems

In *The Right to Complain* (DSS 1991) the Social Services Inspectorate (SSI) argues that complaints systems should:

- be accessible to users, their carers and representatives;
- be understood by staff;
- guarantee complainants and their representatives a prompt and considered response;
- provide a strong problem-solving element.

They go on to propose four principles for an effective complaints system. Senior management *commitment* is essential and should be demonstrated on a day-to-day basis. This may mean allocating responsibility to a senior manager or regular monitoring reports to committee or full council. The report argues that 'the spirit in which complaints procedures are implemented will largely determine their effectiveness'. The system should be *accessible* and user-friendly. It is important to remember that some groups in the community are particularly vulnerable and feel themselves powerless in relation to the local authority. The complaints system should not disadvantage them further. *Communication* is a vital part of accessibility. This can range from the provision of leaflets to mentioning the complaints procedure in all contacts with customers or citizens. Finally the organisation should provide clear

Figure 5.10: Complaints and the management process

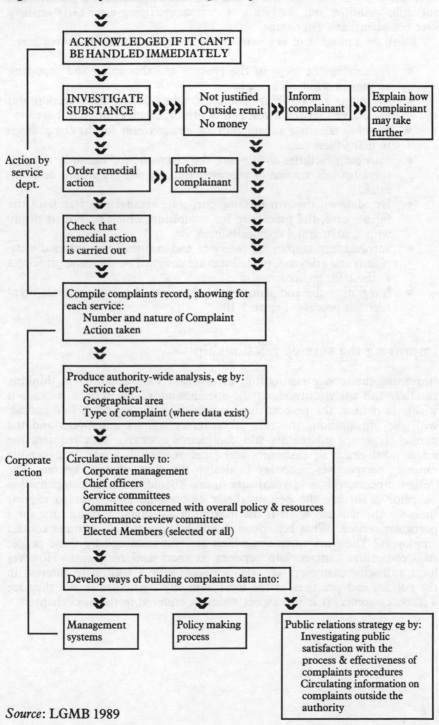

Source: LGMB 1989

information about what services it can and cannot provide, its policies and allocation priorities and the rights of customers. Being clear early on may save complaints at a later stage.

There are a number of key issues in the design of the formal procedure:

- Identifying the steps in the process and the action and reporting arrangements at each stage.
- Allocating responsibility for the conduct of any investigation and the power that the investigating officer, member or team have.
- Enabling adequate and appropriate arrangements for the complainant to make their case.
- Providing facilities to support the claimant, for example through specialist information or representation by outside groups or advocates.
- Deciding on departmental or corporate arrangements and, in the former case, the procedure for complaints which do not sit neatly with departmental responsibilities.
- Safeguarding employees' interests and ensuring that internal complaints and grievance procedures are designed on the same principles as those for customers and citizens.
- Integrating the complaints procedure into the organisation's management process (Figure 5.10).

Improving the service relationship

Improving the service relationship involves the local authority in thinking carefully and analytically about the specification of the service package it wishes to deliver, the process through which customers come into contact with the organisation, the role of customer contact employees and the nature of service guarantees and complaints systems. This requires the active involvement of customers and employees at all levels, bringing the range of perspectives necessary to design the most effective system. The design process will raise many questions: should financial compensation be paid? What are the best methods of enabling customers to express their dissatisfactions? What is the maximum acceptable waiting time for a particular service? What behaviour should be expected of customer contact employees? These are questions which are best answered by those people who come into contact with services as users and recipients. However local authority customers are also citizens with a legitimate interest in the policies and practices of the local authority – whether or not they are a direct customer. It is this aspect which is explored in the next chapter.

6 Councillors and citizens – the political dimension

Taking service quality seriously implies more than the adoption of customer care approaches (see Chapter 2). Customers are also citizens and consequently have a dual relationship with the local authority – as an influencer and a recipient of local authority activity. However while consumerism in the public sector can help local authorities think of those whom they serve as 'customers with legitimate rights and preferences . . . it will rarely be enough to turn (them) into partners, actively involved in shaping public services' (Potter 1988, p.157). Elected members have a key role in this respect as their public status and ward, party and council responsibilities make them a focus of attention for citizens, customers and pressure groups, although in many authorities they have been little involved in service quality initiatives.

This chapter explores a range of issues to do with the essentially political relationship between citizen and local authority and highlights the practical implications for those engaged in improving service quality. The chapter initially discusses the role of elected councillors and the way in which their contribution to service quality can be enhanced. It then takes a wider perspective by reviewing the ideas of citizenship and empowerment and discussing the approaches local authorities can use to strengthen the contribution and influence of citizens and customers.

The elected member's role

Elected members provide a key link between the local authority and its community. During the electoral process people express their views to candidates in door-to-door canvassing and at meetings. Once elected councillors will be involved in discussions with citizens, customers and local party members about ways of dealing with particular issues. On committees and in full council the elected member will be making judgements about the policies of the authority and ensuring that they are implemented as intended. They will attend meetings with particular groups – a tenants' association, pre-school play-group or senior citizens' club. Finally as a ward representative the councillor will be in touch with constituents about a wide range of matters. From telephone calls, surgeries and personal contacts the elected member builds up an understanding of issues which are of concern to the community and how they are affected by the authority's policies and services.

Since service quality affects all aspects of the authority's work it is vital that elected members are fully involved and that their role is developed to the full. In its recent report *Customer Care: A Guide for Elected Members* the ADC (Association of District Councils 1991) identifies ways of achieving this.

1. Strengthening the ward member's role. Members often have little opportunity to discuss the range of issues affecting their ward and consider how the authority could respond. An annual meeting of councillors from one or a group of neighbouring wards with the officers delivering services to that area provides one model. This forum might also involve representatives from other relevant agencies. Political decentralisation or community councils involving local residents and having a small budget, as in Middlesbrough, provide alternative possibilities (see Chapter 7).

2. Strengthening the authority's focus on particular customer groups. Making use of councillors' information and knowledge about particular groups could lead to member/officer working parties to review services to one group of customers. Alternatively elected members could be involved in information-seeking or consultation meetings. Some authorities have gone further and created standing committees or sub-committees to advise on ways in which services across the whole council could be made more responsive, for example Leicester City Council's Pensioners' Advisory Committee.

3. Bringing customer information into the policy-making process. While members have their own sources of information they have limited time and resources. Routine surveys and research will provide a representative picture of views across the community, complementing members' own understanding and officers' professional advice. It increases the authority's ability to make decisions which are responsive to the needs and wishes of the community.

4. Monitoring complaints and praise. Systematic monitoring of both praise and complaints can give members (and officers) a much clearer view of the performance of the authority, of the areas where it is perceived as doing well and the services which could be improved. At present issues raised in members' surgeries are often dealt with on a case-by-case basis. Systematic monitoring of concerns raised by constituents with elected members would provide an additional perspective on the authority's service quality.

5. Clarifying the member/officer relationship. The organisation is not always designed to reflect the full range of the members' interests. Appropriate opportunities to discuss ward issues or service performance, for example, may not be available. Local authorities should develop appropriate structures to facilitate the member's interest in and contribution to service quality. This might involve devoting time at committee to considering the quality of particular services or creating panels to provide a customer focus.

6. Designing service quality initiatives with member involvement. In reviewing services and developing approaches to build better

relationships with customers, use should be made of elected members' contacts and knowledge. In this way the local democratic process will be strengthened rather than bypassed or weakened. Elected member involvement is also important since opening up the local authority may raise a new series of demands and pressures on resources which only councillors are able to resolve.

Some local authorities have established member structures to give service quality initiatives a focus. These include member-level working parties and sub-committees of policy committee.

- Stroud District Council's Customer Service Sub-Committee has embarked on a programme of customer service reviews. This involves service sampling by committee members prior to a presentation by the relevant manager and a representative group of employees on ways in which that section or facility are implementing the council's customer service policy.
- In Leicester the Leader chairs a customer care working party comprising councillors and chief officers. This reviews strategy and performance on service quality and identifies priorities for future action.

It is important to remember that improvements to member support services also have an important contribution to make. Easier typing, message taking and research facilities can make a considerable difference to the councillors' ability to do their jobs and hence improve service quality for customers and the community's relationship with their elected representatives and the local authority as a whole.

Involving people in the political process

It is through lobbying, protesting and the electoral and political processes that citizens seek to influence councillors to make particular decisions. This political dimension is an important aspect of the concern for service quality since it reminds the local authority that customers are also citizens with a legitimate interest in and right to influence decision-making. Active citizenship however also involves empowerment – the ability of groups and individuals to take effective action on their own behalf.

Citizens and citizenship

Citizenship involves rights and obligations on both the citizen and local authority which are of a more fundamental nature than customership. Indeed it sets the context within which the customer/provider relationship takes place. Authorities therefore need to consider their stance towards citizens and citizenship when developing strategies for service quality.

Stewart approaches this by focussing on the nature of local government itself. He defines a citizen as:

a member of a community which governs and is governed by the local authority. A citizen is part of local government. The citizens vote and it is citizens to whom the authority is accountable. A citizen has the right to be an active participant in the affairs of local government (Stewart 1988, p.59).

He then states a series of citizenship entitlements:

- to know the policies of the authority;
- to know the decisions of the authority;
- to know the reasons for the policies and decisions;
- to be able to debate and discuss the issues that the council is considering;
- to have their voices heard on issues which are before the council and on issues which should be before the council;
- to have their interests and concerns weighed by the council;
- to be involved in the governing of the local community;
- to take part in decision-making;
- to mould the work of the council;
- to judge the work of the council;
- to vote.

It is rare for any of these to be covered in current local authority service quality initiatives. To increase awareness of citizenship issues the *Commission on Citizenship* established by the Speaker of the House of Commons has recommended that 'local government officers . . . should have specific training on the entitlements and duties of citizens and the corresponding obligations of public institutions as set out in such documents as the European Convention' (Stonefrost 1990, p.xix). Local authorities might also start by taking an outsider's view of their own proceedings. Here is a citizen's eye view of a council meeting:

There are no signs to announce it. The public gallery is up six steep flights of stone stairs. The minutes and other papers for the meeting are an inch thick. There are no explanations for members of the public. It is difficult to see or hear. Councillors have microphones and still shout 'Speak up!' It is a large room with a high, decorated ceiling, wood panelled walls and rich red carpet. Opposite the public gallery are long beige curtains with the borough coat of arms. A long wooden table stands on a dais with a massive leather backed mayoral chair. Opposite are banks of varnished desks for the councillors. It is both luxurious and reminiscent of a crown court. The meeting starts promptly at 7.30. 'Be upstanding for his worship the Mayor.' 'Good evening Councillors.' His Chaplain then leads the Council in prayer starting with a reading from Leviticus (Croft and Beresford 1989, p.9).

This picture is not unique. In another local authority, otherwise committed to improving service quality, the public gallery is reached by climbing several flights of stairs having previously gone through some tall wooden gates around the corner from the main (councillors') entrance, walked down a narrow courtyard and through a door under a dimly lit sign announcing 'Strangers' Gallery'!

Because few local authorities have seriously considered the nature of citizenship or developed strategies to enhance it the rights of citizens remain obscured. Consequently the image of an impenetrable political process in which citizens need to mobilize huge amounts of energy in order to achieve any degree of access or influence is often experienced as the reality. As discussed below, some local authorities are now treating this issue seriously and taking steps to encourage and be more receptive to citizenship rights.

Empowerment

Empowerment has become a catch-phrase of the service movement in local government. Many talk of the need to empower employees, customers and citizens. However one observer comments:

> Most advocates of consumerism have so far left the idea of empowerment at an entirely rhetorical level. Participation and accountability as espoused in local government notions of consumerism do not necessarily imply any real shift in the distribution of resources . . . and the term empowerment has often been a heady substitute for policies which would bring about any changed practices or structures, or reveal any real commitment to partnership (Berry 1988, p.270).

Empowerment involves individuals or groups increasing their ability to take effective action on their own behalf. This might include:

- an individual having increased confidence to ask for a service, challenge a decision or speak at a public meeting;
- a group organising around an issue and presenting their case to the local authority.

The Adam Smith Institute (1991) argue that the empowerment of public sector customers should involve financial compensation or the automatic right to use another service (possibly provided by the private sector). This approach, however, ignores the wider question of empowering people as citizens and in that respect takes a narrow view focussed purely on individuals as customers. The concept of empowerment therefore covers a range of activities but at its core is people's increased capacity to have greater influence over the way in which local authorities and other agencies relate to them (Meade and Carter 1990).

In order to develop effective strategies for empowerment it is important to understand two key aspects of the relationship between community and local authority. The first is the nature of local authority power and the different aspects which it has. The second is the process through which demands and issues pass before they are formally considered by the local authority.

Local authority power as a constraint

The local authority can choose to impose considerable constraints on the power of its citizens and customers by doing no more than the legal minimum. This would mean that citizens could vote and would have their statutory rights in relation to particular services, for example to be consulted on planning decisions and to be provided with information under the Access to Information legislation. And the local authority might do no more than that. Individuals and groups could write letters, march in demonstrations, lobby councillors and take direct action yet would have no influence on the decisions or practices of the local authority. The organisation would remain unmoved, labelling the protesters as 'unrepresentative' or 'self-interested' or 'only a few hot-heads'.

Local authority power operates at three levels. The most visible is *service power*, regulating access to existing services in terms of opening hours, rationing criteria, speed of response and information systems. It is service power, often through its expression in the gate-keeper role of customer contact employees, of which customers and citizens tend to be most aware. At a second level is *strategic power*, the power to define, structure and resource a service in a particular way. This power is applied in the formal and informal policy-making processes of the local authority and through the interaction of senior managers, elected members and those outsiders with privileged access. It is strategic in the sense that it sets the context for action and results in a particular pattern of resources and stream of lower-level decisions. It is the exercise of strategic power that determines the availability and standards of service for customers. At a deeper covert level the local authority has considerable *structural power*. It can choose those voices to which it listens and those it ignores – are business interests, gypsies and travellers, local authority tenants, women and landowners all actively involved in local government or are some excluded? It can determine the issues to which it will respond and their relative priority and those matters it will ignore.

This analysis has two main implications for local authorities developing empowerment strategies. Firstly local authorities often assume that they are part of a pluralist political environment – in other words that the local authority is a benign and impartial institution which acts as the umpire between competing sets of interests all of whom have an equal opportunity to express their views. This perspective assumes that power is not concentrated in one or a few hands but distributed throughout the local political system. The practical experience of some groups of citizens and customers as well as studies of local government in action suggest that this is not the reality. Access to and influence over the local authority's policy-making process is open to some and closed to others and while there may be changes at the margins, such as the greater involvement of environmental groups in recent years, there are some who are always 'insiders' and others who are always 'outsiders'.

Secondly it is important to address all three levels of power and provide opportunities for citizens and customers to gain access to each. While individuals or groups may initially be concerned with the authority's service power and influencing changes at this level, the process should enable them also to contribute effectively in terms of strategic and structural power. Indeed it may well be that challenges to the structural power of the local authority are a necessary precursor since it is here that groups' acceptability is determined.

Explaining non-involvement

Local authorities sometimes initiate community development or consultation programmes only to find that people do not want to be involved or that a high level of public participation is not sustainable. This can lead to frustration and annoyance on the part of officers and members who feel that they are doing what they have been told people want, yet get little response. Some reasons for this were discussed earlier (Chapter 3). There is, however, another explanation. In order for an issue to get to the point of a local authority making an explicit decision it must pass through a number of steps or filters. At each stage people may decide not to pursue the issue further (Figure 6.1).

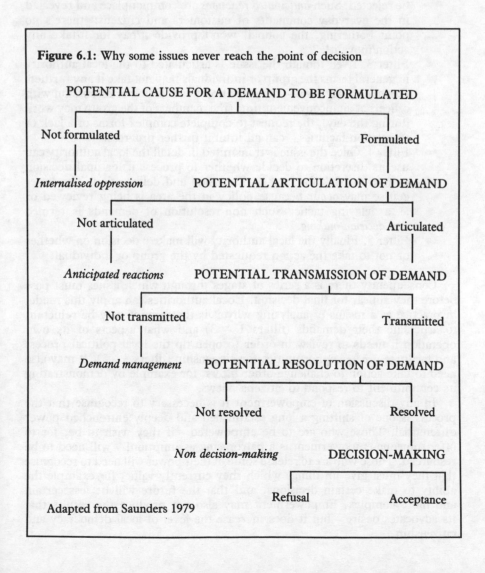

Figure 6.1: Why some issues never reach the point of decision

POTENTIAL CAUSE FOR A DEMAND TO BE FORMULATED

Not formulated   Formulated

Internalised oppression   POTENTIAL ARTICULATION OF DEMAND

Not articulated   Articulated

Anticipated reactions   POTENTIAL TRANSMISSION OF DEMAND

Not transmitted   Transmitted

Demand management   POTENTIAL RESOLUTION OF DEMAND

Not resolved   Resolved

Non decision-making   DECISION-MAKING

Refusal   Acceptance

Adapted from Saunders 1979

- Filter 1. At the most basic level an issue may not be identified even though, to an outside observer, there is cause for the individual or group to do so. This is because the socialisation processes particular groups go through and the 'taken-for-granted' assumptions in society as a whole result in people failing to recognise their real interests. This is termed *internalised oppression*. For example the past failure of public agencies to think about physical access to their buildings combined with a socialisation which stressed that disabled people should be 'grateful for what they got' resulted (until recently) in relatively few demands for improved access being formulated. Access difficulties were accepted as the norm.
- Filter 2. Having identified an issue the group may decide not to articulate it to the local authority because they believe that it will be rejected. Such *anticipated reactions* are commonplace and revealed in the everyday comments of customers and citizens: 'there's no point bothering, the council won't provide it/pay for it/take any action/move it'.
- Filter 3. Even though the issue is articulated to the local authority in general terms the group or individuals may not take it any further. *Demand management* – the invitation to a meeting or discussion with officers at an inconvenient time (the members of the group may work during the day), the request to complete complex forms or a lack of translation facilities – can all inhibit further progress.
- Filter 4. Once the issue is transmited in detail the local authority can use its discretion to decide whether to process it for final decision or refer it back for further discussion and deliberation. The latter course may occur because policy in the area is being reviewed or as a delaying tactic. Such non-resolution of demands is termed *non decision-making*.
- Filter 5. Finally the local authority will make a decision on whether or not to take the action requested by the group or individual.

Consequently there is a series of stages through which issues must pass before they appear for final decision. Local authorities can apply this model in practice as a means of analysing why it is that groups may be reluctant to articulate their demands (filters 1 – 3) and what aspects of its own operation it needs to review in order to open up the local political process and facilitate greater opportunities for citizenship (filters 3 – 5). It may also need to take action to challenge other filters, for example by demonstrating its commitment to respond to citizens' views.

In any discussion of empowerment it is necessary to recognise that the process is one of shifting a long established and deeply entrenched power differential. Those who are to be empowered – if they wish to be, for to offer someone empowerment is a patronising assumption! – will need to be resourced. Those who are to release some of their power will need to recognise that they must give up things which they currently value, for example the ability to make certain decisions, and that the future will be less certain and more complex. Empowerment may also not produce the results that its advocates desire – but it does increase the level of local democracy and citizenship.

Approaches to empowerment and citizenship

While some strategies to empower citizens and customers have a long history and tested techniques and skills – for example community development – others are only now being developed in practice. This is a new area for many local authorities and the methods and experiences will only fully emerge in the next few years.

Community development

Community development is one approach to empowerment. It aims to assist groups and individuals to identify their common interests and take a more active part in shaping the decisons that affect them. Many local authorities employ community development workers or people who have a similar role, usually in the housing, social services or leisure departments. Community development covers a multitude of activities:

- assisting a group of parents to establish a pre-school playgroup;
- supporting residents in a particular area to organise and press for environmental improvements;
- working with an Asian community to find funding for and run a drop-in centre for older people;
- identifying individuals who can provide sports training for a group of young people;
- helping a tenants' group understand the procedures of a local authority so that they can more effectively press their demands for a policy on bad neighbours.

A recent report (AMA 1989, p.7) highlighted three principles which are central to any community development activity:

- Firstly, it is based on the ability of people to act together to influence and assert control over social, economic and political issues which affect them...Community development aims to effect a sharing of power and create structures which give genuine participation and involvement.
- Secondly, community development is about involving the skills, knowledge and experience of people in taking initiatives . . . This will usually involve cooperation or negotiation at some level with statutory agencies.
- Thirdly, community development must take a lead in confronting the attitudes of individuals and the practice of institutions which disciminate against . . . disadvantaged groups.

By enabling groups to become more actively involved community development should assist the development of citizenship. At the same time it will facilitate greater responsiveness by local authorities in both service delivery and decision-making; provided that the local authority is prepared to look critically at its existing practices and not discount the views of citizens and customers!

Developing citizenship and empowering customers

Building better relationships with citizens and developing citizenship rights requires local authorities to review critically the nature of their power relationship with the community and consider the extent and effect of different interests' access to decision-making. Some local authorities are taking this step.

- Harlow DC has an initiative entitled 'Getting Involved with Harlow Council'. This involves neighbourhod and issue-based forums, user groups, public question time at council committees and the positive advertising and encouragement of lobbying and petitioning.
- Several local authorities have undertaken campaigns to encourage local electoral registration and early applications for proxy or postal votes.
- *Community action* is an initiative launched by Southampton City Council to increase citizen involvement in decisions. Neighbourhood forums, involving residents, community representatives and councillors, have been established in four localities to highlight local issues and identify changes.
- Financial and other resources can be provided to support groups previously marginalised in the local government process to organise and become more fully involved where they wish to take advantage of this opportunity.

Recent government legislation, especially in the housing and education fields, has been designed to empower customers. Local authorities themselves are also developing other models:

- Croydon social services department provides recruitment and selection courses for customers with physical disabilities, enabling them to take a full part in the selection of employees who will work as their carers.
- Housing estate management boards, such as those being established in Birmingham, give tenants considerably greater power to make decisions about their area and the housing and related services they require.
- Statements of rights (or charters) are being developed by several local authorities. Southwark social services have developed a charter of rights for those living in residential homes for the elderly. Sutton LB has a charter for the under fives detailing the way the authority will involve and take account of the views of those using the service. Humberside has a charter of rights for older people in the county which also contains a statement of rights for carers and employees.

A new local politics

The implications of these developments on existing patterns of local political activity and local government have yet to become clear. It does appear, however, that the traditions and assumptions of representative democracy are being transformed as citizens and customers claim their rights and exercise more effectively their voice in local affairs. It affects also the role of officers as they become more visible and accessible to the community and find that they are expected to become accountable to a wider audience. Finally it is important to highlight that the energy and effort of councillors, citizens, customers and officers in creating a more active local democracy will largely be wasted if the local authority is unable or unwilling to respond to the demands made of it. In this sense the internal organisational and managerial processes and cultures need to adapt to the challenges which they now face as a result of taking customers and citizens seriously.

7 Organising for service quality

Managing for service quality involves managing the organisational arrangements through which the local authority wishes to achieve its aims. Organisational structures and processes can hinder or facilitate the identification of customer requirements and delivery of quality services through:

- inadequate coordination between departments leading to service failure for a group of customers;
- localised service provision increasing customer access;
- absence of managerial responsibility causing delays in decision making;
- effective liason with health and voluntary sector agencies leading to improved joint provision.

This chapter explores a range of organisational choices and their implications for service quality, covering:

- committees and departments;
- strategic approaches;
- decentralisation;
- devolved management;
- client/contractor roles;
- links with the voluntary sector.

The development of service quality is an organisational as much as an individual issue and therefore the design of structures and processes is of particular importance.

Committees and departments – the basic building blocks

The member structure of committees and the officer structure of departments have been the basic building blocks of local authority organisation. They are a way of dividing up the work of the authority into manageable and apparently discrete chunks. Committees operate within a codified scheme of delegation from the full council which in practice permits a considerable degree of autonomy and self-regulation. Typically departments report to a single committee thus forging a strong link between officer and member interests in a particular area of responsibility.

Historically the committee/department structure has emerged from the growth of local authority functions and specialisms, often based on particular professions. In the mid-twentieth century town planning emerged from the engineering and architecture functions and in many authorities became a department in its own right. Similarly in the 1980s, economic development departments emerged from planning and estates functions. Economic development officers now constitute a quasi-profession with their own body of knowledge, association and training programmes. Often committees were established in parallel with the creation of these departments.

Because of this specialisation and professionalisation the traditional committee/department structure offers certain advantages to the authority concerned with service quality. A strong body of knowledge is concentrated at one part of the organisation and professional career structures can be created in order to attract and retain employees. Because departments aim to recruit professional specialists rather than generalists, new developments and learning are constantly being introduced into the organisation and its services. Finally it enables elected members to develop a functional specialism to supplement their ward role.

The advantages of specialist committees and departments need to be weighed against the disadvantages. In particular:

- The dominance of professional interests. Elected members (particularly backbenchers) and customers sometimes feel that they have little influence over or ability to challenge professional perspectives. Reports generated within the departmental structure often arrive before the committee with a recommendation reflecting professional judgement, which in some cases is at variance with the preferences of customers and elected members. Challenges to the professional view are sometimes perceived by officers as 'parochialism' or 'politically motivated' and can be ineffective because elected members have no alternative source of professional advice. The implication for service quality is that the paternalism inherent in professionalism can tend to predominate.
- Departmental loyalty. There is a strong tradition that officers are expected to adopt departmental policy and not publicly challenge it. This particularly affects the many grey areas in implementation where officers themselves are interpreting members' wishes and in effect making policy. The implications for service quality are that debates about different choices and interpretations of members' intentions are not made explicit outside the department and hence do not receive a wider debate.
- Professionals first, managers second. Middle and senior management posts are typically occupied by those with a professional rather than a managerial background. This leads to a tendency for such individuals to perceive themselves as professionals first and managers second. While service quality initiatives require professional inputs, it is often managerial skills that are at a premium in assisting the organisation to change and develop a service quality focus. These

skills may be undervalued or neglected in professionally-based departments.

- Inter-departmental tensions. The creation of specialist departments inevitably leads to divisions in the organisation. In a situation of limited financial resources this can result in competition between departments to protect their budgets and responsibilities and, together with negative stereotypes of other parts of the authority, a lack of willingness to cooperate. Additionally, corporate initiatives on service quality or other issues may be resisted because they do not reflect departmental priorities. Departmentalism can therefore act as a constraint on service quality because interdepartmental activity is required to effect improvements – for example in complaints systems or standards of access.
- Limiting the member's role. The functional organisation of committees and departments can prevent the elected member from operating effectively as a ward representative since there is no forum in which the range of issues affecting the locality can be discussed. There is also no guarantee that individual councillors will be placed on a committee which reflects their particular interests. This further limits the key role of councillors in service quality (see Chapter 6).
- Developing mismatch between structure and issues. The organisational structure is a picture of how the authority perceives the issues it faces at one point of time. As issues change, so a mismatch develops. The recently accepted priority on services for the under fives, for example, has resulted in local authorities devoting considerable energy to articulating appropriate organisational arrangements to unify the separate provision by social services, education and other departments. Such organisational rigidity constrains the dynamic response required if service quality is a core value.

Improvements in service quality therefore require local authorities to balance the advantages and disadvantages of the traditional functional committee/department structure against those of other organisational arrangements.

Developing a strategic approach

While departmental and committee organisation is about dividing up the local authority the strategic approach is about recombining it. The purpose of the strategic approach is twofold:

- to establish effective coordination and liaison between related functions; and
- to ensure that the activities and policies of the authority are all contributing towards corporate objectives and values.

In other words it is both about developing linkages across the organisation and moving the authority forwards in a particular direction. In this sense it is related to the ideas of corporate planning in the 1970s and policy planning in the 1980s.

A strategic approach is essential to an authority seeking service quality improvements since:

- a failure to develop effective linkages between functions or policies is a cause of poor quality;
- corporate direction is necessary in order to develop and implement a strategy for service quality (See Chapter 9).

Within a local authority the strategic approach will have two main elements. Firstly there is the organisational structure which typically includes a policy and resources committee, chief officers' management team and corporate member panels, officer/member groups and officer working parties on key issues. However these organisational forums operate in the context of the second element – a policy process through which issues are identified and explored, choices raised and decisions made, implemented and monitored. Without a well designed and effective policy process the corporate structures will likely be ineffective or a positive hindrance to service quality.

Policy processes vary from authority to authority but typically involve bringing together information on four areas:

- environment – economic and social trends, customer perspectives, physical development changes and the policies and programmes of other relevant agencies;
- politics – the values and policy framework set by elected members, their relative priorities and the preferences of customers and citizens;
- activities – the current programmes and services of the authority, levels of provision and usage and new professional and technical developments;
- resources – the financial, human, physical and other resources of the local authority and the way they are likely to change in the immediate future.

This information is utilised in a structured sequence of events although there may be an overlap or recycling between stages. In many authorities the strategic policy process sets the context for and contains within it the budgetary process and hence becomes the key annual decision-making cycle (Figure 7.1).

Because of the concern with service quality it is important that the process is explicit and visible to customers and employees and that arrangements are made to enable their contribution to the decisions which will result. For a number of years, for example, Coventry City Council has published its draft policy plan and invited comments and views from residents and other interested parties. Similarly Gloucestershire CC circulates its annual corporate review of key issues and priorities to a variety of agencies and individuals asking for comments prior to the next stage of the policy process. The right balance must also be struck between matters of corporate and departmental concern. The corporate focus should be on a small number of key issues rather than a wide range of topics. In particular it should see itself promoting the core values of the organisation.

Figure 7.1: The strategic management process of a local authority

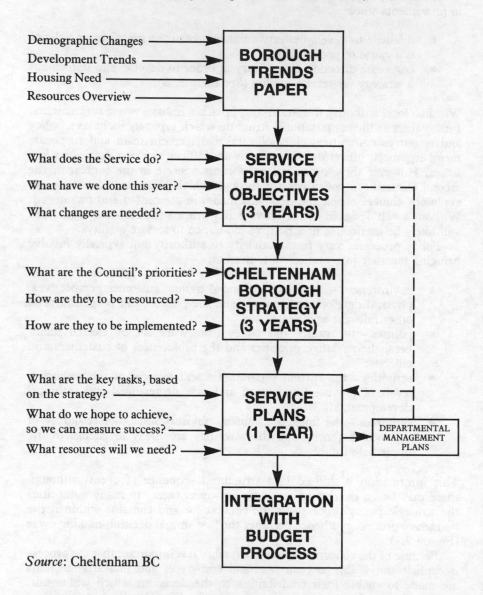

Demographic Changes ⟶
Development Trends ⟶
Housing Need ⟶
Resources Overview ⟶

BOROUGH TRENDS PAPER

What does the Service do? ⟶
What have we done this year? ⟶
What changes are needed? ⟶

SERVICE PRIORITY OBJECTIVES (3 YEARS)

What are the Council's priorities? ⟶
How are they to be resourced? ⟶
How are they to be implemented? ⟶

CHELTENHAM BOROUGH STRATEGY (3 YEARS)

What are the key tasks, based on the strategy? ⟶
What do we hope to achieve, so we can measure success? ⟶
What resources will we need? ⟶

SERVICE PLANS (1 YEAR)

DEPARTMENTAL MANAGEMENT PLANS

INTEGRATION WITH BUDGET PROCESS

Source: Cheltenham BC

Close to the customer – decentralisation and service quality

The allocation of responsibilitiies between and within departments sometimes has little apparent rationale when viewed from the customer's perspective:

- Why does the environmental health department deal with house improvement grants rather than the housing department?

- Why can't housing benefit and community charge rebate be dealt with at the same office?
- Why do trading standards and environmental health departments both deal with food complaints but have different responsibilities and work from different offices?

Redesigning the organisation from the customer perspective has led a number of local authorities to decentralise to area or neighbourhood level.

Administrative decentralisation

Authorities have undertaken administrative decentralisation by establishing local offices. While in some cases these may be an access point for one council service (for example, housing or social service) in others a variety of functions are represented at this level. Decentralisation has a number of objectives related to service quality:

- Improving physical accessibility. The aim is to establish access points for council services close to where people live so that they do not have to make long journeys to centrally located council offices. Personal visits can also be made rather than relying on impersonal telephone calls.
- Creating a customer-friendly climate. Neighbourhood officers are typically designed and staffed in a way which helps create a less bureaucratic and formal environment. Open planning and locating employees within the sight of customers are common.
- Improving service delivery. The higher level of personal contact between customers and local authority employees is intended to build a greater commitment to improved service delivery, with neighbourhood office staff in some cases acting as advocates for customers in their dealings with other parts of the authority.
- Single point of access. The intention is that the neighbourhood office should provide a 'one stop shop' giving access to as many of the department's or authority's services as possible. Because customers tend to make personal visits to the office rather than phone in, they can also see who is dealing with their enquiry and recognise them on any return visit. The anonymity of local authority employees is thus reduced and 'pass the customer' less likely to happen.
- Developing a corporate approach at the service delivery level. Administrative decentralisation offers the prospect of greater understanding and cooperation between departments and sections because employees working in the same office or neighbourhood have greater contact with each other and a more specific focus on service delivery to customers. Some authorities are also aiming to develop a range of generic skills amongst neighbourhood office staff.

Administrative decentralisation is not a panacea. It has costs as well as benefits. It requires capital expenditure on new or refurbished neighbourhood office buildings and computer systems to link the offices with each other and central departments. Effective training programmes are essential to provide employees and managers with the skills to undertake new roles. There will be a degree of organisational disruption in the transition to a decentralised system and its settling in period. Industrial relations issues may also be significant with employees unwilling to transfer from centrally located and large offices to small outposts which may not be close to shopping or social facilities. Political and managerial commitment is a key condition to the successful implementation of a decentralisation scheme, particularly when it involves a number of services across the authority. Local authorities should have a clear implementation plan and be able to ensure sufficient support from members and managers over the critical initial period. These managerial, financial and human resource implications of developing a decentralised system should be seen in the context of the improved service quality achievable by this form of organisation.

Political decentralisation

A few authorities have decentralised their political structures and established area committees or non-statutory community councils. The intention is often to provide a forum where councillors representing that locality can meet to discuss the range of issues affecting the area and gather opinions and information from residents. Birmingham's area sub-committees (which reported jointly to the council's Finance and Management and General Purposes Committees) covered groups of wards and had an advisory role. This structure has now been replaced with single-ward sub-committees. Some authorities have created area committees for a single service. In Walsall MDC the Planning Committee has area sub-committees to consider issues relevant to each locality. Middlesbrough DC's community councils, each covering a specific part of the borough, consist of councillors as well as representatives of local interests and are an integral part of the council's policy process.

The role of such committees may be purely advisory, reviewing proposals from main programme committees in the light of local circumstances. A small budget could be available to fund environmental improvements or local voluntary groups. Alternatively executive responsibilities may be delegated. This is the case in Tower Hamlets where there has been a major programme of decentralisation to seven neighbourhoods, each of which has a neighbourhood committee and sub-committee structure responsible for extensive financial, policy and service decisions.

Political decentralisation can have major benefits for service quality because of the way in which it offers opportunities for

- elected members to play a more active role in the range of issues affecting their ward and its residents;
- resource allocation and service policy decisions to be made more sensitively in relation to the needs of specific localities;
- customers more effectively to exercise their role as citizens because of greater access to political processes and decision making forums.

It can, however, make explicit underlying tensions and conflicts since locality becomes a counterweight to the functional bias of the traditional local authority committee structure. Choices therefore are no longer mainly between service areas but also between neighbourhoods. The Tower Hamlets model seeks to resolve this by establishing locality as the key factor. In any event new methods of resolving the tensions inherent in a system which is both functional and decentralised will need to be established.

Devolved management – letting managers manage

In Search of Excellence argued that two of the criteria exhibited by successful organisations were:

- a bias for action; and
- close to the customer (see Chapter 1).

Local authorities have often not scored highly on these criteria. This is partly because the process of government involves discussion, negotiation and compromise, but is also due to the low priority customers have had, the remoteness of many managers from the point of service delivery and the bureaucratic nature of local authority processes. At the same time as excellence has become a goal for some authorities politicians have become concerned about the nature of managerial accountability and have sought to link managers' responsibilities more directly to political objectives agreed by the council and its committees. The result of these two pressures has been the development of devolved management. This is a global term which also encompasses what some authorities refer to as accountable or cost-centre management.

Devolved management is a logical extension of the strategic management process. Indeed its starting point is the establishment of overall policies and priorities. These are then translated into targets or key tasks for individual managers. Managers are given greater discretion over the way financial and other resources are used to achieve these targets. In return they are also held accountable for their performance and that of their unit through periodic reporting to higher levels in the organisation who may exercise sanctions or provide rewards. One local authority (who use the term management delegation) see the changes and their benefits in these terms:

> Management delegation is about enabling managers to make the decisions appropriate to their level of responsibility. It means the top of the organisation concentrates on strategy, overall performance and key tasks whilst cost centre managers at the point of service delivery are entrusted with the tools to make operational decisions. It means giving cost centre managers the authority to use the resources that have been allocated to their areas of responsibility and it removes detailed constraints on individual decisions. However it does not mean the abdication of responsibility by top management. Management control is exercised through clear lines of accountability based on explicit objectives, targets and procedures for monitoring and review (Warwickshire CC 1990).

Improvements to service quality are therefore perceived as one of the key benefits of devolved management initiatives. Establishing such a system requires local authorities to resolve three key issues.

What to devolve to whom?

Devolved management rests on the assumption that quality reduces the further the point of service management is away from the customer. The corollary is that the maximum degree of delegation should take place to the lowest appropriate level in the organisation. Typically local authorities with devolved management systems identify those sections or units which are the smallest that can be sensibly managed as an entity. This could include the discretionary awards section in an education department, an equal opportunities unit, a children's home or a training and development section. The next step is to decide what the managers heading these units are to become responsible for. The local authority needs to make decisions about four main issues, the first two of which are also frequently found in performance related pay systems whether or not part of a devolved management system:

- Accountabilities. These are the enduring aspects of the managers' job and might include a responsibility for ensuring an efficient service, providing annual performance reports to committee or monitoring customer satisfaction.
- Targets. By contrast targets or key tasks will be set annually, often as part of the formal appraisal process, and tend to be specific and quantifiable – for example increasing income by 5 per cent, processing 90 per cent of planning applications within eight weeks or responding to all complaints within seven working days.
- Resources. One of the key elements in a devolved management system is the transfer of responsibility for resources to managers. This means more than just providing improved financial information to cost centre managers. It involves giving managers the freedom to use the resources at their disposal in the most effective way to achieve their targets. This could include:

  - Discretion over the pay and conditions of employees. Managers may be authorised to pay additional increments or honoraria subject to remaining within the overall cost centre budget, or vary hours or other conditions of employment.
  - Virement within the budget. This might be between heads within the year, for example transferring from the building maintenance account to purchase new equipment, or the ability to carry over underspend from one year to the next.
  - Obtain competitive tenders for work to be undertaken by contractors. Cost centre managers can be released from the requirement to use in-house suppliers of catering, building, financial and other services and given the discretion to obtain a range of quotations from internal and outside sources.

- Service policy. The concept of devolved management suggests that managers are given greater discretion in the way they interpret policy and that elected members and senior managers withdraw from the specification of administrative and implementation details.

Cost centre managers are therefore left to implement policy in the best way they can identify, consistent with resource constraints and their accountabilities and targets. However the dividing line between policy and administration is unclear. Implementing policy can itself have political implications. A leisure centre manager with a target to increase income by 10 per cent might decide to gear provision towards high demand/high income generating sports such as squash or roller-hockey and away from those where the financial returns were not so great, for example keep fit for older people or mother and toddler sessions.

What is the role of the centre?

These issues inevitably raise questions about the role of the 'centre' of the local authority – the elected members, senior levels of management and corporate functions. Not only will a number of their responsibilities be delegated to lower levels of the organisation but – and this particularly applies to the central support services – they will operate in an internal market where cost centre managers have greater power because of service level agreements and (sometimes) the ending of the obligation to purchase support services internally. Cost centre managers become customers too and look for improvements in service quality from internal suppliers.

In this situation there are several ways in which the centre can respond, each of which involves a different type of relationship between it and cost centre managers:

- Strategic planning. Here the centre establishes a small number of core values which it incorporates within the devolved managers' accountabilities and expects to see reflected in services. The centre works with these managers to assist them to develop their strategies within the available budget and provides ongoing support. The way in which managers are assessed places more emphasis on the extent to which they have reflected the core values than kept to their annual financial targets.
- Strategic control. In this model cost centre managers themselves produce plans which are then appraised and prioritised by the centre. From its own work and the analysis of cost centre plans the centre sets strategic and financial targets. The expectation is that managers achieve their financial targets unless there is an important strategic issue at stake, in which case the exception reporting system would highlight it for decision by the centre.
- Financial control. Here the centre is concerned primarily with the short term and with achieving financial targets. Once the cost centre managers' annual budgets are approved they are expected to be able to manage within them. Severe penalties will be enforced if budgets overshoot the agreed limit (Goold and Campbell 1987).

The role of the centre can therefore vary from the definition of core values and a facilitative approach in working with devolved managers to a concern with ensuring that cost centre managers obtain the most value from their budgets and on no account overspend. Paradoxically devolved management can involve tight control by the centre – but only of a small number of variables. The danger of the financial control approach is that the concern with managing budgets may detract from service quality as managers spend more time concentrating on their actual and projected expenditure than the needs of customers. Improvements in service quality may also require an increase in expenditure which may not be possible within a financial control regime. Indeed one of the disadvantages of devolved management is that it places the responsibility for service quality on cost centre managers operating within a budget which they feel may not be sufficient for the task. The centre therefore has a responsibility to ensure that the service quality implications of the budgets set for cost centres are assessed.

Whatever approach the centre takes it still has the key task of determining the budgets for cost centres. This can be undertaken on the basis of historical levels of expenditure, bids and negotiations or a formula. Each has advantages and disadvantages (see Figure 7.2). The centre must also decide whether it wishes to retain a corporate pot to fund special initiatives or seed-corn work in priority areas. This might, for example, be available to fund service

---

Figure 7.2: Methods of allocating finance to devolved budgets

1. Past expenditure
   - may be desirable/unavoidable in the short run
   - defensible as outcome of collective decision-making
   But . . .
   - rather conservative
   - no guide to coping with change
   - not always easy to measure in practice
   - inequitable

2. Bids/plans/negotiation
   - involves bottom-up participation
   - brings special local problems to attention
   - obliges local management to engage in analysis, planning, etc.
   - copes well with lumpy capital projects
   But . . .
   - encourages over-bidding and tactical bidding
   - time consuming in developing and appraising bids
   - generates much information and paper
   - may increase central control/influence
   - appraisal criteria or techniques may be limited
   - may be inequitable

3. Formulae
   - explicit criteria and methodology
   - apparent fairness
   But . . .
   - may be seen as over-technocratic
   - may be too crude or incomprehensible
   - still have to make choices about principles/criteria
   - data may be inadequate

Source: adapted from Hoggett and Bramley 1989

quality improvements identified by customer contact employees. Finally the centre must decide how to treat under and overspends. Should cost centre managers be able to retain 100 per cent of any underspend as a means of encouraging further value for money improvements? Or 50 per cent, the remainder returning to the centre to fund any contingencies or overspends in other areas? Or none of the underspend on the grounds that the resources ultimately belong to the authority as a whole?

What is the nature of sanctions and rewards?

Devolved management systems require a mechanism by which managers can be held accountable for their performance and can convey to the centre information which is of strategic significance for the authority. The process should enable a full review to be undertaken of:

- managers' progress in meeting the targets set for the period;
- exceptional circumstances which caused any variation;
- key issues identified for the next period, including those requiring action by the authority corporately;
- suggested targets for the next period.

The full annual review could be supplemented by half-yearly or quarterly progress meetings. The most common format is for managers to be assessed by their immediate superior with the results subject to confirmation by the latter's manager (or elected member depending on the level of manager). In the case of dispute this individual would also hear any appeal.

A number of rewards and sanctions are used in devolved management systems. The regular publication within the organisation of managers' performance against target or budget provides a source of moral pressure on poor performers and public recognition of the stars! The difficulty is that it can create a climate of antagonism and unhealthy competition and fail to recognise that 'poor' performance may be due to circumstances outside the manager's control – for example a severe winter disrupting road maintenance targets. An alternative is for the centre to take a closer interest in those managers regarded as not performing satisfactorily and in some cases withdrawing the freedoms they enjoy as cost centre managers. Management development and other training may be used to bring poor performers up to standard or as a reward for good performance.

The most common method of sanctions and rewards is pay. Alternatives to the traditional incremental salary scale are now becoming more common in local government and elsewhere in the public sector. Many senior managers have a variable performance related bonus as a supplement either to the traditional incremental scale or a fixed term contract at an enhanced salary or a salary linked to that of comparable private sector managers. Previously such performance related bonus systems had been applied solely to manual workers. A banding system is often used with the level of performance related bonus being determined by the assessor's view of the manager's performance (see Figure 7.3). The severest financial penalty is often the withholding of both the bonus and annual increment (where the manager is on an incremental scale).

Figure 7.3: Banding system for performance related pay

Band	Salary Change
1	5 – 10%
2	1 – 4%
3	increment
4	nil
5	action required

Source: LACSAB 1990b

The recent LACSAB review of PRP in local government commented:

> Repeatedly it was said (by individuals in local authorities) that PRP had 'sharpened up performance', or encouraged 'greater dynamism' or that 'it forces you to do good things' . . . What stood out from several of these accounts was a conviction that PRP was not raising performance because a cash incentive was motivating people to work harder . . . What was said to be raising performance was the performance review procedure. The main benefits of this were that it improved communication between employee and manager, clarified principal objectives and led to more focussed work activity (1990a, p.59).

The study also found that many managers shared their PRP amongst their staff either as a direct payment or to fund some collective benefits. They took this action from a recognition that this bonus was produced through collective effort, but were also aware of the divisiveness created by PRP systems which apply only to certain (usually senior) levels of staff.

These conclusions are particularly important for local authorities concerned with service quality. They indicate that good management practice in the form of employee development or appraisal systems will themselves increase performance and that the personal reward offered by PRP is of limited value. The implications of this analysis are developed in Chapter 8. A further question is where the finance for PRP comes from. In some authorities managers are expected to fund their PRP from within their own cost centre budgets. Even though the amounts involved are small such a method can have considerable symbolic significance and give rise to a view of managers benefitting at the expense of the service.

Client/contractor and purchaser/provider – the impact on service quality

The separation of roles between the client (or purchaser) and the contractor (or provider) is now widespread as a result of CCT and community care legislation. Each role has specific responsibilities. The client:

- undertakes market research and other analysis to determine the need or demand for the service;

- specifies the service required on the basis of the analysis, political, professional and customer priorities and financial availability;
- competitively or otherwise lets the contract;
- monitors the contractor's performance against the specification and other contract conditions;
- takes appropriate action where necessary to ensure contract compliance;
- makes payment for the work undertaken.

The contractor has a more limited role which is essentially to fulfill the contract specification and other conditions to which they have agreed. In practice this basic client/contractor split can become more complex. For example in a county council education will be the largest single client for the grounds maintenance service, others being the highways (for verges), social services (in terms of residential establishments) and property (for main council offices) departments. In this situation a lead client in one of the larger client departments is often identified, although the detailed specification might be written by each individual department who would also undertake the day to day contract monitoring through their employees – the caretaker, highway inspector or head of establishment (Figure 7.4).

Figure 7.4: The organisation of the client function

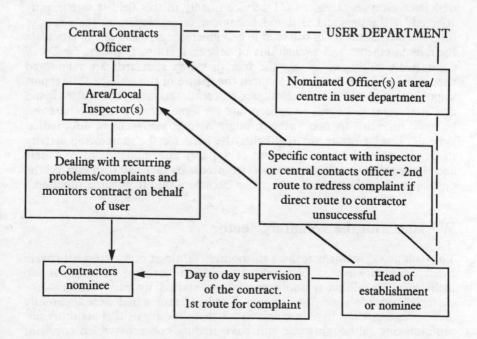

Source: Walsh 1991

In terms of service quality the separation of client and contractor roles provides a number of benefits. Firstly it requires local authorities to specify explicitly the service it wishes to provide, something which has seldom been undertaken to any great degree. Secondly it clarifies the responsibilities and resolves the potential role confusion between those managing and those delivering the service. The client can concentrate on what it wants provided and leave the contractor to deal with the delivery. Thirdly it focusses attention on monitoring and inspection. A key role for the client is to assess the performance of the contractor against the specification and in this sense someone in the organisation is concerned with the level and quality of service to the final customers in the community.

There are however disadvantages to the client/contractor split. In his review of the first year of CCT, for example, Walsh (1991) highlights three main issues:

- Increased cost due to the need to establish a client side for the monitoring and management of contracts.
- Additional organisational complexity. Officers in user departments can no longer go directly to the contractor to have additional work undertaken, but must first contact the client officer. The lead client structure can also create additional bureaucratic complexity.
- Potential antagonism between client and contractor especially where the contract specification and conditions are poorly drafted.

With the introduction of purchaser/provider splits into social services a new issue emerges. Unlike CCT service quality in this field is significantly affected by the personal skill and behaviour of employees in the provider role. Further, many users will tend to be vulnerable and less able to articulate their requirements and evaluations of service quality. *Contracts for Social Care* (AMA 1990) argues that the way in which standards are monitored should therefore be designed to match the nature of the activity. The report suggests that such 'softer' techniques as consumer surveys, regular liaison and assessment visits will be appropriate for some services while others will be more amenable to monitoring through 'harder' management information systems. Finally the report highlights the need for the monitoring activity to be integrated into the provision of support and guidance to providers and the ongoing identification of service needs. In this way it should aid the development of the service rather than become a purely policing function.

Working with the voluntary sector

The 'voluntary' sector is really a misnomer. While at one extreme it covers small community associations run by unpaid and part-time volunteers it also includes multi-million pound organisations staffed by paid workers – for example Barnardo's and Age Concern. The key features that these apparently diverse organisations have in common are that they are neither statutory nor profit-making (although some will have trading concerns which covenant their profits back to the parent organisation), that they have charitable or quasi-charitable objectives and that they provide services and facilities for the community. Local authorities have a long tradition of financial support for the voluntary sector although until the 1980s this tended to involve relatively small scale grants or payment for specific services. Many local authorities, especially in the metropolitan counties and London, have strengthened and expanded their relationship with the voluntary sector in recent years. However this source of funding for the voluntary sector is discretionary and so always at risk in times of budget constraint.

Developing a relationship with the voluntary sector has particular benefits for the local authority concerned to improve service quality (Gutch *et al.* 1990). This is because voluntary sector organisations typically are:

- Responsive – customers are often involved in the management or delivery of the service and thus the organisation becomes more responsive to their needs
- Innovative – having no statutory roles or duties they can be created as and when individuals feel it is necessary, and to undertake those activities they feel are important in whatever way they choose. This can provide models for subsequent adoption by local authorities.
- Cheaper – compared with local authorities, many can provide services at lower cost because they rely on voluntary labour and donations of materials
- Networkers – because many are an integral part of particular communities they have extensive networks which can provide information, skills or contacts not normally available to the local authority.

Working with the voluntary sector may therefore have particular benefits where the local authority is seeking to:

- provide quality services in an activity or to a customer group where it lacks expertise – for example a centre for the Vietnamese community;
- develop and monitor an innovative pilot project – for example community management of an environmental improvement scheme;
- gain access to the views of a group of customers – for example working with a tenants' association in undertaking a survey;
- review or coordinate services to a particular customer group – for example in reviewing services to older people in rural areas;
- facilitate the provision of a small-scale service at a number of points across the authority – for example grant-aiding voluntary playgroups.

The nature of that relationship can be one of partnership, principal/agent or rival. *Partnership* implies that voluntary sector and local authority work together in providing services and resources to their local communities. It recognises the different strengths that each has and seeks to utilise and coordinate these to the maximum advantage of customers. *Principal/agent* involves the voluntary sector providing services on behalf of the local authority. This increasingly includes a form of contractual relationship and may involve the voluntary sector competing for some tenders offered under CCT. As local authorities review their relationship with the voluntary sector conditions of grant aid are becoming more concerned with what the agent will achieve with the funds rather than just the procedural checks so common in the past. Finally the two sectors may be *rivals* working in an uncoordinated or even antagonistic way. This model can arise because of the failure of a local authority to recognise and appreciate the different culture, traditions and conventions of the independent voluntary sector.

At the heart of the relationship will be resources. Buildings, equipment, information, access to the political process and the secondment of local authority employees may all be important – but often finance will be the key. Three choices are available to the local authority:

- Core funding. This is not tied to any specific project or service but is designed to enable the voluntary organisation to finance its basic administrative, training, development, management and overhead costs. It is usually much easier for the voluntary sector to attract one-off revenue or capital monies and those for specific projects. Such ongoing revenue funding of their core activities is therefore particularly important and enables them to increase the quality of the service they offer.
- Project funding. This is tied to a specific activity or need identified by the voluntary organisation. It could fund the repair of a community centre or an information project on keeping warm in winter targeted at older people. Such grants may be one-offs or pump-primers designed to start the project and assist the organisation to find financial support from other sources in the future. The difficulty for the voluntary sector however is that alternative sources of funding often are not available.
- Service funding. This involves the local authority paying the voluntary organisation for the service it provides. Meals on wheels may be delivered by the WRVS with the local authority paying x pounds per meal. A Vietnamese community association may provide translation services for which the local authority pays a fixed rate. This type of funding will often be regulated by some form of contractual agreement.

The voluntary sector provides a number of advantages for local authorities interested in service quality. Developing the relationship, however, requires an awareness of the many different ways in which such organisations operate. It also requires a clear strategy established in partnership with the voluntary sector. While the voluntary sector in a local authority area may be able to provide the benefits listed above, they may also have shortcomings which affect their ability to deliver quality service. The NCVO and other agencies are now devoting considerable energy to improving the capacity and skills of these organisations and those working in them. The local authority should also be aware that some sections of the voluntary sector find it more difficult to obtain funding than others. Black and ethnic minority groups, advocacy groups and advice agencies often face severe funding difficulties yet provide essential services and support to their communities. Targeting of support is therefore important. Finally local authorities need to take care that the development of the contract culture does not squeeze out the variety of formal and informal support offered to voluntary organisations – free or subsidised transport and buildings, technical advice and training resources. These are invaluable resources for voluntary organisations.

Options for organisation

In most local authorities departmental and committee structures remain the prime way of organising. However there is a wide range of practical examples of the other approaches discussed in this chapter, many operating as a complement to the departmental approach. In addition there are other methods of organising, including:

- companies with a local authority interest;
- management buy-outs;
- charitable trusts;
- employee cooperatives.

These models are explored in detail in *A Local Authority's Options for Service Delivery* (LGMB 1990, see also Brooke 1989). The LGMB report recommends that local authorities evaluate different methods of organising against a series of criteria (Figure 7.5).

Figure 7.5: Criteria for choosing an appropriate organisational arrangement

1. Assisting the authority to understand the service need
2. Ensuring realistic economy and efficiency
3. Delivering effective, quality services
4. Equality of service delivery
5. Experience, knowledge and resources of the existing providers
6. Openness to monitoring
7. Directness of accountability and control
8. The client/purchaser's knowledge and experience
9. Flexibility of response
10. Management culture and values
11. Employer concern for staff and their future
12. Local authority and employee capacity to make the change.

Source: LGMB 1990

Organisational redesign is not the sole solution to the problem of poor service quality. Frequently, however, it is seen as the easiest solution – a common expression of hope is: 'once the structure's right then everything else will fall into place'. Structures are important but so too are the processes which give them life. Developing service quality requires more than just changing organisational arrangements. It has a wider managerial agenda which is discussed in the next chapter.

8   Service quality – the management agenda

Customer satisfaction surveys, improving reception areas, better information and publicity, establishing user groups – there are a range of initiatives that local authorities can undertake to improve their relationship with customers. Yet these will make little overall difference to service quality unless the organisation itself and employees at all levels within it have the capacity, resources and motivation to respond to the new climate of 'customer first'.

Building internal quality is the key. Some local authorities have adopted quality assurance as a technique for achieving this while others are developing total quality management. Both are discussed in this chapter. Whether these or more incremental approaches are adopted attention should be devoted to four areas. First, establishing clear connections between the front-line of customer-contact employees and the back-line of support staff so that the latter can assist the former to deliver the authority's services to the standards set. Secondly, the ability to achieve high levels of service quality is affected by the information, skills and resources of employees, and therefore their development is particularly important. Thirdly, managers have a key role in encouraging and supporting employees' initiatives and improving the quality of relationships within the organisation. And finally, attention must be paid to the organisational culture and the way in which this facilitates or inhibits service quality.

Quality systems – a comprehensive approach

A number of local authorities have taken a comprehensive approach to improving service quality by developing quality assurance (QA) and total quality management (TQM) systems. These offer the prospect of greater customer satisfaction, the reduction or elimination of errors and faults and more efficient and productive internal working practices and procedures. Before discussing QA and TQM it is helpful to set them in the context of quality control (QC), a more traditional and widespread approach to quality management.

Quality control is an inspection and checking process which occurs after the service has been or is ready to be provided. Its purpose is to identify actual performance against desired standards and as a result provides information on the error or failure rate of the service. Sometimes quality control takes place before customers use or receive a service, for example testing the chemical content and temperature of a swimming pool before opening time or managers reading and signing letters written by their staff. In other cases, particularly where the service is produced through the personal interaction of customer and provider, quality control can only take place after the event. Examples include tenant satisfaction surveys following a housing repair and peer assessment of an environmental health inspector's performance.

If the implicit purpose of quality control is to stop mistakes or sub-standard performance from happening again, that of QA is to get it right first time and every time. It involves designing the systems and procedures of the organisation so that performance against the specification is guaranteed and quality (in this sense of the term) is always delivered. Many local authorities are developing QA systems, particularly for existing DSOs and DLOs, trading standards, design services and leisure. The National Health Service is also extensively involved in establishing QA systems, with many health authorities and units having a QA manager. British Standard 5750 is the recognised benchmark against which local authorities can assess their QA systems and a number are now formally accredited with the British Standards Institute. QA originally developed in the manufacturing sector where products can be specified in technical and quantitative terms and objective measures utilised. In local government this is seldom possible to the same extent. Consequently careful thought about the application of BS5750 standards is necessary and some adaption may be required.

Introducing a QA system involves four main steps. Initially the service has to be designed. This involves the review of existing provision, possibly involving consultation with customers, employees and other interested parties, and the specification of activities to be undertaken and standards or levels of performance to be achieved. Secondly, the policies and procedures involved in producing and delivering the service are fully documented in a quality manual. This will include the allocation of responsibilities, monitoring procedures and control systems. Thirdly, employees are trained to fulfill the requirements laid down in the QA manual, including any additional specialist skills they require to operate it correctly. Finally the system is audited to ensure that it operates correctly and that quality is assured. It typically takes two to three years to work through this process and arrive at an accredited QA system (AMA 1991).

All local authorities will have some form of quality system, often of the quality control type. While QC is cheap and easy to implement, its main disadvantage is that the customer may first have to suffer from poor service (see Figure 8.1). For example, in residential homes for children or elderly people the absence of QA has enabled physical and emotional mistreatment of customers to take place. While quality control through random and unannounced inspections may reduce the incidence of such events it is no guarantee that standards will be met each and every time. Additionally QC does not guarantee that clear and explicit standards of performance and procedure are in place. Quality may be controlled against personal or partial parameters. QA necessitates the codifying of policies, procedures and perfor-mance standards and guarantees that these will be met. However developing QA can be a resource intensive activity and involve fundamental changes in the organisation's systems and culture. Further, quality is defined in terms of performance against specification. If the specification is inappropriate and fails to meet the needs or expectations of customers they will not define the service as a quality one – whether or not it is BS5750 accredited. It is essential that local authorities have the correct service design and specification if QA is to mean anything.

Figure 8.1: Quality control and quality assurance – an assessment		
	Quality Control	**Quality Assurance**
	Applicable in all service areas	Requires clear service specification
	Easy to implement	Links to employee motivation
Advantages	Generally simple to use	Improves value for money over the medium term
	Cheap	
	Customer may first experience poor quality	Expensive and time consuming to develop
Disadvantages	May be established in absence of adequate service specification	BS5750 needs adaptation for some services
	Management information generated may not be utilised	No guarantee specification is what customers want

It is managers' and employees' commitment to quality – to getting it right first time and every time – that is essential for a QA system to work. Without this commitment the quality manual will be perceived as a bureaucratic encumbrance, at best a chore to be followed and at worst an impediment to be subverted. In this respect the development of a culture of quality is essential and hence TQM becomes the corollary of QA. BS5750 is defined in terms of procedures and systems but for it to operate effectively requires the development of a culture of quality in the organisation.

TQM is an approach to improving the effectiveness and flexibility of business as a whole. It is essentially a way of organising and involving the whole organisation; every department, every activity, every single person at every level. For an organisation to be truly effective each part of it must work properly together, recognising that every person affects, and in turn is affected by, others. TQM is a method for ridding people's lives of wasted effort by involving everyone in the processes of improvement; improving the effectiveness of work so that results are achieved in less time (Oakland 1989, p.14)

The TQM methodology varies from author to author – Crosby, Oakland, Deming – but essentially involves the organisation and individuals within it internalising the commitment to quality and letting this value shape their perceptions and actions. TQM therefore bears on the organisation's:

- overall strategy;
- organisational form and allocation of responsibilities;
- recruitment, selection and induction processes;
- design of organisational processes;
- inspection and recording systems;
- teamwork, employee development and communication.

Everything the organisation does should therefore be designed from a quality perspective and the message of quality be reinforced at every point. Some of these elements have been discussed earlier in the book; others are explored in the rest of this chapter.

Front-line/back-line relationships

One of the key features of TQM is to focus attention on the internal customer relationships which contribute to serving the external customer. Quality in the former is perceived as essential to achieving quality in the latter. This involves exploring the relationship between the front-line, those employees in customer contact roles, and the back-line who support them in this task and assist them to deliver the authority's policies and services.

The most appropriate analogy to use is that of a chain. All the links in the chain need to be right before it can do its job and the same is true of the local authority – all the parts need to be performing their role and the connections need to be strong before quality service can be delivered. This applies whatever the type of decision. For a home help to deliver her service to the highest quality she needs a number of others in the organisation to operate effectively:

- her supervisor – to give support and advice;
- the training section – to effectively convey skills and knowledge;
- the finance department – to pay her wages and expenses promptly;
- research section – to provide information on new services and voluntary organisations;
- managers and members – to secure the resources, policy and organisational framework necessary to provide a quality service.

The same is true of a local authority committee making a decision on resource allocation between competing priorities. It relies on professional advisors (to give accurate information on the consequences in a form which is easily digestible), finance department (to have calculated the relative levels of expenditure accurately) and the committee clerks (to get the papers out on time – provided the officers writing them keep to the delivery dates!).

Clarifying the front-line/back-line relationship and responsibilities is a key element in the design of the service package (James 1989). As with any organisation local authorities face weak links in their internal service chains. Often this is ascribed to personalities – someone is perceived as being difficult to work with or incompetent. While individuals do have different levels of expertise and skill it is important also to take a wider perspective.

The structure, culture and resourcing of the organisation can have as much if not more impact on the ability to deliver good internal service. There are a number of approaches to establishing stronger internal service chains, some of which are outlined below. However, much can also be achieved through employee development initiatives.

Developing employees

Employee development in the context of service quality has a number of components:

- the induction process;
- skill development;
- quality initiatives;
- equalities initiatives.

In their first few days and weeks new employees discover much about the organisation, what it stands for and how it operates in practice. They will be socialised into established ways of perceiving and behaving towards other parts of the authority and groups of customers which may or may not be in accord with the values of good service quality. In those authorities where induction training is offered it sometimes takes place weeks or months after joining the organisation and therefore may have little impact compared with the subtle, day-to-day socialisation process to which the new employee will have been exposed. Its content frequently fails to convey information on the values of the organisation and the importance of service quality, confining itself to terms and conditions of employment and related matters. Thinking seriously about the induction process as a whole, including induction training, is essential for authorities wanting to change the practices of the organisation and its employees.

- Several local authorities now ensure all new employees start on the same day each week and follow a carefully designed induction pro-gramme for their first two or three days. This often includes a coffee or buffet lunch session with the chief executive or service director, presentations on the authority and its role and values, initial training on service quality and customer contact and an element related to the specific job the employee will be undertaking.
- All employees joining Birmingham City Council's neighbourhood offices undertake a one week residential induction programme which explores the purpose and role of the neighbourhood offices, systems and procedures and issues related to customer contact.

To be effective employees need the skills and information to enable them to undertake their job properly. However workforce surveys such as those undertaken by Services to Community Action and Trade Unions (SCAT) have consistently highlighted manual and clerical workers' feelings that training provision is *ad hoc* and inadequate. It often requires a supervisor or manager to take positive steps to identify training needs and search out suitable provision, a more difficult task when local authorities see the training budget as an easy cut in periods of financial constraint. As a result service quality suffers. Skill training for individuals and work-groups is a vital investment in the future and a clear strategy is required in order that it can deliver the results in improved quality.

- Derwentside Housing Department closes its offices every Wednesday afternoon for employee development activities, including training, service reviews and briefings on current developments. Managers and elected members may be involved in this process.
- As a response to CCT skill development training for workforces has been increased in a number of authorities, a central aim being the delivery of a higher quality service.

Recently there has been considerable interest in quality initiatives which actively involve and help develop employees. These include service days and quality circles, bringing together employees and managers working in one part of the organisation to identify blockages to quality and plan ways of overcoming them. A central feature of these activities is that by working together people in different parts of the service chain can build a fuller understanding of the service process of which they are all part and themselves formulate and agree improvements. These events often result in the creation of a quality group who take responsibility for identifying and implementing further initiatives.

Such training and development on quality should not be seen in isolation. *Quality and Equality* (LGMB 1991) has highlighted the need to integrate equality into training related to service quality. It argues that a focus on customers inevitably involves a consideration of discrimination, prejudice and disadvantage and that these issues should be addressed in service initiatives. Work is only now developing in this field. Some authorities, for example Wolverhampton MBC and Watford BC, are making equal opportunites an integral part of their customer care training packages.

Service quality – the manager's role

Managers have a key role in developing service quality. Their leadership can help create a climate for quality. They can use their authority to overcome blockages and initiate changes. Their access to information and other resources are invaluable in developing new ways of doing things. Their managment style can support employees and assist them to identify and make quality improvements. Managers have an essential and substantial contribution to make in the movement to improve service quality.

For many managers this is unfamiliar territory. The traditions of local government have been to promote those with strong professional competences into managerial positions. Yet the introduction of service quality initiatives and the other changes facing local government require skills and abilities that are essentially managerial: understanding and analysis of new situations; developing and conveying a vision; mobilising resources to develop solutions; negotiation, persuasion and the exercise of influence;

recognition of the human, organisational and political dimensions of change. This is illustrated in a recent study of the management of the housing service:

> The management quality of local housing office managers is a key determinant of service quality. Local office managers who spent less time working on the details themselves and who felt least threatened by the extra call from an elected member or the extra demand for yet more statistics from the centre . . . were generally those who could cope and manage best. They also had other characteristics. They had their own vision of how the local estate should be managed that was often independent and sometimes opposed to that of the centre. They found their own priorities. They tried to get the office to work together as a team, they set time aside regularly for reviews of how people's work was progressing, they kept closely in touch with other area housing officers and with housing officers at the centre . . . Generally they had stronger instinctive or learnt 'people management skills' rather than 'housing management skills' *per se* (Walsh and Spencer 1990, p.52).

How employees see managers

Several authorities have begun the process of identifying current management capacity and planning future development by undertaking consultation exercises or attitude surveys with employees.

- Kent CC commissioned MORI to undertake an employee opinion survey. Working with a project group of officers, trade union and departmental representatives and drawing on an earlier qualitative study for the authority, self-completion questionnaires were sent to all 47,000 employees. The questionnaire consisted of core questions to be answered by all employees together with supplementary ones relevant to specific departments. A 46 per cent response rate was achieved and initial results were circulated to all employees. The results have also been presented to members and are being taken forward in a number of ways.
- East Kilbride DC, working with Market Reseach Scotland Ltd., conducted a survey of customer and employee attitudes. The employee survey covered career history, education and training, communication and morale, corporate image, customer demands and employee satisfaction. It highlighted the strengths and weaknesses of the organisation but also revealed that employees consistently underestimated customers' satisfaction with the council. This is a finding that has been reported in other authorities.
- Gloucestershire CC undertook a review of its staff development interview process (an annual appraisal interview between manager and employee). To facilitate open discussion the three managers responsible for the review held consultation meetings with employees grouped according to their level in the organisational hierarchy: scale 1–3, scale 4–6, SO, PO and senior management. A separate meeting for black and ethnic minority employees was convened. Separate meetings

for women were not held because almost all employees on scales 1–3 and 4–6 were female. Clear confidentiality groundrules were set at the beginning of the meetings. In addition a postal questionnaire was sent to all non-teaching members of the Education Department, achieving a 37 per cent response rate. The consultation exercise gave information not only on the staff development interview process but the role and behaviour of managers generally.

The evidence from employee attitude studies indicates a number of ways in which internal relationships could be improved and those at lower levels in the organisational hierarchy enabled to deliver higher quality service to their customers.

Employees tend to have a strong belief that *their work makes an important contribution* to the authority and its services to the community. There may be frustrations and irritations but overall local government employment is seen as worthwhile. Authorities engaging in improvements to management capacity and service quality are therefore starting with a positive attitude on the part of employees. The ability of employees to do their jobs to the best of their ability, however, requires a clear understanding of what is expected of them and how their jobs fit into the overall picture. Many employees feel that this is missing and that *downward communication could be improved*. Informal channels such as the grapevine or office gossip are frequently a main source of information and are often quicker than formal systems. However staff prefer meetings, circulars and discussions with managers. This is not just because grapevines distort information but from a positive preference to hear directly and face-to-face from those who are making decisions which affect them. Employees also *value feedback on their performance* combined with the opportunity to discuss and review their jobs and the way in which they do them. However they do not feel that sufficient time or attention is given to this task by managers. Even in formal staff appraisal systems interviewees frequently feel that managers come unprepared, poorly skilled and fail to afford them sufficient priority.

Employees often experience communication as a one-way process – downwards! There is a strong feeling that *insufficient opportunities exist for them to let management know* what they think or feel and that their views are not taken into account when important decisions are being made. Where there is an opportunity to express opinions and ideas they seem to disappear into a vacuum since no feedback is given on what has subsequently happened. This is perceived not solely as an issue for individual managers but an organisational problem rooted in the culture and traditions of the institution.

Finally employees at lower levels in the organisation frequently say that *their experience is of being systematically devalued*. Appreciation, recognition and thanks from higher levels in the hierarchy are rare. They do not believe that managers really understand the issues and situations employees face nor the impact on them of managerial decisions or behaviour. They feel their skills and intelligence are not fully utilised to the benefit of the authority and its customers. Status differentials are keenly felt and the apparent flexibility and discretion of the professionals' and managers' working days noticed and compared with the tighter controls on clerical and manual employees.

It is noticeable that self-evaluation surveys of managers reflect a number of these issues. A survey of almost 200 senior and middle managers in Kent CC revealed that they thought they:

- were good at goal setting but poor in communicating goals to employees;
- measured things that were important to managers but not things which affected or frustrated front-line staff;
- ensured customers knew all the services that were available but were poor at using front-line staff as a source of ideas and skills on customer service;
- believed they 'lived the customer message' but were not so good at communicating it (Webster 1991, p.51).

The consistency in employee attitudes across those authorities who have sought to survey them (remembering that these authorities are often the most progressive in management terms) suggests that the problem cannot be put down to a few incompetent managers. Rather it is a structural issue to do with the way in which managers are trained and developed (or not trained and developed!) and the impact of organisational culture, particularly the way in which power and status are ascribed. The significance of this latter point is sometimes discounted by managers who fail to recognise that employees in lower status or non-managerial posts frequently perceive them as having considerable ability to influence the nature, type and location of their work and their promotion prospects. For this reason staff meetings and one-to-one discussions with managers may not always result in employees being as open as they would like about the issues which concern them.

Employees as customers: the impact on managers' roles

Strategies to improve service quality as well as other changes affecting local authorities are redefining the relationship between employees and managers. Local authority managers are having to develop the skills to support and facilitate employees at lower levels in the organisation to develop their own solutions to quality problems. Employees are thus becoming the customers of managers' skills, resources and access. Managers need to serve their staff well in order that these staff can serve their customers in the community or (for central services) other departments.

This has two key implications. Firstly managers must establish the service package which their staff require of them. Just as local authorities traditionally did not seek out and identify the views and needs of their customers so managers have not explicitly explored what their staff require. This is the challenge which they now face in the authority committed to service quality. The discussion in Chapters 2, 3 and 5 is therefore directly transferable to managers' relationships with their employees. Secondly a different style of leadership is required. Traditional models of leadership are built around two roles – the leader and the follower. In a situation of devolved responsibility and authority it is more appropriate to think in terms of leaders leading leaders. The key task of those occupying formal positions of leadership (managers and supervisors) becomes to release the leadership potential of those who work for them:

- to inform employees so that they understand the wider context within which their job is located, including the values of service quality;
- to facilitate the development of their skills and confidence in making decisions and taking steps which are beyond those traditionally expected of them;
- to support them in resolving the issues they face, particularly where their actions are perceived as 'mistaken';
- to appreciate their contribution and create a climate in which positive recognition of effort is widespread;
- to assist their learning throughout this process.

It is a role for which most managers have not been trained and involves risk-taking. The temptation to intervene and make decisions for employees will be strong but must be resisted. Building quality within the organisation requires pluralism rather than the dominance of particular groups and perspectives.

Local authorities are establishing a number of mechanisms to assist the development of their managers. In addition to course-based management development activities there are:

- Secondments – internally as well as to other organisations. This enables managers to widen their understanding and skills by working in new environments with different types of problems and ways of responding.
- Management clubs. These include regular meetings of managers to discuss issues of common concern, often with outside speakers, newsletters and other methods of information exchange.
- Women managers' groups. These provide an opportunity for women managers to explore the specific issues they face working in a predominantly male environment.
- Cross-professional career development. Some local authorities en-courage managers to apply for posts in other departments as a means of developing general management skills and spreading good practice across the organisation.

These should be seen as elements in a strategy to change the culture of the organisation since they will not necessarily in themselves have a significant impact. There is also a danger that without similar facilities for other groups of employees they merely reinforce the status distinctions which already exist.

Developing a service culture

Joining a local authority involves a process of socialisation into its culture. The culture of the organisation has a number of elements:

- the unwritten and taken-for-granted rules about how the organisation operates and how to get things done (or stop them occurring!);
- the nature and quality of relationships between individuals and across levels in the hierarchy or departments;
- the informal but real distribution of power in the organisation.

Typically cultures in local authorities and other institutions have reinforced the power and status differences between groups. For example the culture may say something about whether secretaries and managers can use first names when talking to each other or whether only the manager is permitted so to do. The culture can therefore accentuate or moderate formal differences in power and status. In other cases the culture may reflect forces in society at large. Prevalent assumptions about people who are HIV+, together with other negative stereotypes, can affect the way in which employees who are openly gay are treated by their collegues. The key point is not that differences between groups are bad *per se*, but that the cultural perspective through which these differences are perceived often:

- is based on slim or incorrect information;
- devalues the contibution or needs of one of the parties; and
- hinders the effective working of the organisation and delivery of quality services to internal and external customers.

Stereotypes are central to the socialisation process. They are strong taken-for-granted beliefs which mascarade as statements of fact. They can assist a group to become cohesive by presenting an image of the differences between itself and others but also have a number of undesirable consequences:

- They are often wrong. Stereotypes frequently derive from myths, anecdotes about specific instances and misinformation and propaganda conveyed by one group to discredit another. This is clearly demonstrated in the way in which black people have been portrayed in Britain over several hundred years (Fryer 1984), but also applies to a range of other groups.
- They are used by those with power to define the worth of others. There are stereotypes about all groups but their significance is the way in which they are employed by those with power. In service delivery the power of the local authority has combined with stereotypes about women, people with disabilities and other groups to produce discriminatory decisions. This outcome is also found in personnel and employment practices and decisions. Those at the receiving end typically have less resources to take action and must also work against a dominant power structure and set of stereotypes.
- They are divisive. Stereotypes divide groups from each other in an unhelpful way. They tend to emphasise the differences in a negative light – there is an underlying assumption that 'our' qualities are better or more desirable than 'yours'. Rather than valuing the differences between people and groups, for example the way in

which customers, manual workers, clerical workers, managers and councillors bring equally valid but varying perspectives on how the street cleansing service could be improved, there is a tendency for one or two views to predominate. The combination of stereotype and power devalues the potential contribution of some groups.

The socialisation process has three main stages. Initially those with power identify the difference between themselves and other less powerful groups and propogate stereotypes to support their greater status: for example 'manual workers have no commitment to the job whereas professionals do'. Power is then used to encourage individuals and groups to accept the dominant stereotype of themselves and others and reflect this in their behaviour. For example, training, equipment and employment conditions for manual workers are not given a priority by the organisation and requests for improvements are not acted on. As a result some manual workers become demotivated and begin to behave in line with the stereotype. Finally those rejecting or challenging the stereotypes or the behaviour expected of them are marginalised, penalised or discounted. Within organisations it is common to hear comments such as:

- 'Yes, I know she does an excellent job cleaning our office but she's the exception.'
- 'He's a well known troublemaker. He's just stirring up the others.'
- 'If only they'd show a bit of commitment I'd be more willing to listen to their requests.'

Developing a service culture involves action directed at each of the three stages of the socialistion process (Figure 8.2). Many of the steps suggested can be undertaken by an individual manager or supervisor while others involve changes in organisational procedures or the commitment of a wider group. The most immediate and straightforward steps to take involve validating differences. This involves countering stereotypes and the poor and false data on which they are based by providing accurate information in an appropriate way and recognising the positive contribution of groups who are devalued in the existing culture. For managers this may involve increasing their knowledge and understanding. It could involve taking time to find out more about the needs and experiences of particular groups of customers or employees. For example, white managers working in a multi-racial community should have a good awareness of the different cultures, traditions and histories of groups in the area so that they can see and articulate the reality behind racist stereotypes.

Modelling or demonstrating alternatives to 'the way we do things here' is a second step. This might include creating opportunities to involve those who have previously been excluded or giving greater responsibility and authority to those perceived as having little to offer the organisation. In doing this managers should remember that support and encouragement are essential. Developing employees' skills and capacities and changing the culture is a long-term project. People need time to check out whether there is real commitment to the change process and a crucial indicator is the consistent and solid support of the manager. All members of the organisation will have

Figure 8.2: Achieving culture change by influencing the socialisation

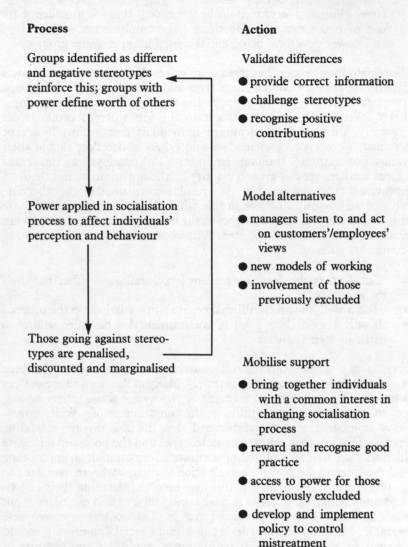

Process

Groups identified as different
and negative stereotypes
reinforce this; groups with
power define worth of others

Power applied in socialisation
process to affect individuals'
perception and behaviour

Those going against stereotypes are penalised,
discounted and marginalised

Action

Validate differences

● provide correct information
● challenge stereotypes
● recognise positive
  contributions

Model alternatives

● managers listen to and act
  on customers'/employees'
  views
● new models of working
● involvement of those
  previously excluded

Mobilise support

● bring together individuals
  with a common interest in
  changing socialisation
  process
● reward and recognise good
  practice
● access to power for those
  previously excluded
● develop and implement
  policy to control
  mistreatment

experienced past management initiatives, sometimes introduced with little consultation and soon abandoned. They will be asking themselves:

- 'Is this for real?'
- 'Can we trust them?'
- 'Do they mean what they say?'

Employees also need time to develop and express their ideas and understand the political context; this needs support and the resources of time and money.

Mobilising support is the final component. Developing a service culture is about redefining the relationships between groups. In this process some will feel that they are losing power, others that they are taking a risk by accepting the invitation to play a more active part in the organisation. Networking and other support mechanisms organised by and for particular groups have an essential role to play and may require management to allocate a small budget or allow facility time. The recognition and reward of good practice (as defined in terms of the service culture) encourages different forms of behaviour. However it is also important to establish effective policies and procedures to counter the mistreatment of one individual or group by another. Sexual and racial harassment procedures and methods of dealing with violence against employees are therefore integral to the service culture.

- Receptionists in Warwickshire CC produced a receptionists' charter which sets out the responsibilities of managers – to provide induction training, keep receptionists informed of organisational changes and developments – and of receptionists.
- A group of employees from different departments and grades in Cardiff City Council were commissioned to produce an analysis of the organisational culture, its impact on employees and service delivery and recommendations for change. This has influenced the management strategy for the organisation.
- A number of local authorities have supported the creation of black workers' groups and women employees' networks as part of a strategy to develop the organisation's culture and provide the opportunity for all employees to make a full contribution.
- Following violence against an employee a local authority has provided a minibus service to transport secretarial, clerical and other staff from their outlying car park to the council offices.

Managers and service quality

Developing service quality involves a range of management skills, some of which have not traditionally been utilised in local authorities. The evidence is strong that a management revolution is necessary to complement and support the revolution in local government's approach to customers and citizens. Without this transformation in management practice, attitude and behaviour, the contradictions between how the organisation treats customers and how it treats employees will be too great and the former will suffer. For managers the key maxim is: treat your employees in the way you would wish them to treat customers.

9 Strategies for service quality

All the time, at various places in our organisations, people are taking steps to improve service quality. Some initiatives will be small and taken by one or two employees while others will be major and involve a considerable part of a department or local authority. For example:

- the librarian who invites customers to join employees in a service review day;
- the park-keeper who notices that wheelchair users have difficulty gaining access to a bowling green and constructs a simple ramp out of some spare timber;
- the supervisor who instigates a weekly half-hour meeting with staff to highlight service quality issues that need to be addressed;
- the women employees who continue to request action to improve customer and employee safety despite management indecision;
- the managers who are committed to a customer perspective and seek to change the paternalistic culture and practices of their local authority by introducing new ideas and approaches.

A survey of any local authority will reveal many such initiatives, all making an important contribution to improvements in service quality. However these contributions are constrained because they are fragmented and rely on individuals taking the initiative in organisations which are often already overstretched and have limited financial resources. As a result resistance to change can be significant, employees with ideas about quality improvements become isolated, disillusioned and demotivated and the good practice developed in one part of the organisation fails to be transferred to other departments or sections. This laissez-faire approach is not the most effective for those many local authorities who wish to develop a customer orientation (see Chapter 1). A corporate decision to get closer to the customer and/or the citizen requires corporate action: it cannot just depend on individuals deciding to instigate change where they see a need, even assuming that they have the power so to do!

A strategy for service quality is essential as a means of implementing corporate intentions and supporting individual initiative. Both elements are important:

- at a corporate level the authority should have a clear set of values pertaining to service quality and an understanding of what changes it expects; and

● at the same time individuals should be encouraged to take additional steps to improve service quality in their own area of responsibility.

There may be issues on which extensive corporate activity is required, for example customer care training or market research, but the strategy should also foster and facilitate employees' own quality awareness and actions. The easiest way to erode employees' commitment and halt the initiative they are already showing is to create a detailed and comprehensive master plan for service quality. The strategy therefore needs to balance corporate direction and action with individual discretion. This is reflected in local authority examples:

Kent's (management) style . . . is about getting on with things and fine tuning later, the 80/20 rule, risk-taking, giving people room to do their best. If you're serious about customers you have to do this. Improvements in customer service are about lots of small wins, not one big change. We encourage and expect our managers to be outward looking, future-oriented, enabling not disabling, and pro-active (Frater 1990, p.354).

Many improvements are best left to individual committees and departmental managers to develop proposals suited to their particular service and client requirements. But there is a need for corporate recognition of the need for better service, and some improvements are central to the function of the council, or require corporate agreement of a framework to enable departments to develop the details (Cheltenham BC 1990, p.1).

Sometimes a strategy will be formulated at the start of an authority's formal concern with service quality. Wrekin DC's customer strategy, established in the mid 1980s, has two main themes: creating a customer-oriented culture within the organisation and improving the quality of service to customers in the community. Each theme is translated into a series of specific initiatives which have become part of the way in which the organisation operates (Figure 9.1).

Figure 9.1: The Wrekin customer strategy – an overall framework

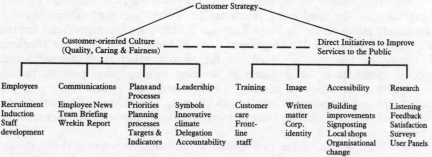

Source: Hancox *et al.* 1989

On other occasions the decision to prepare a strategy provides an opportunity to review existing activity throughout the organisation and plan future action in a more coordinated way. In Leicester City Council a variety of initiatives had been undertaken over several years but on an *ad hoc* and fragmented basis. In 1989 the council established a member/officer customer care working party which audited existing projects, identified those requiring corporate action and encouraged those departments that were least well developed to learn from other more advanced ones. The working party now regularly reviews departmental progress and establishes priority corporate initiatives on an annual basis. (ADC 1991)

The strategy process

The term strategy often conjures up an image of voluminous documents produced over a long time period and having little bearing on the real day-to-day work of the organisation. A strategy, to be effective and helpful, should be selective in what it covers, produced over a short time scale and involve those who it will affect.

The strategy itself should focus on four key questions:

- What are our values? The strategy should involve the definition of values or objectives in relation to service quality. This might be undertaken by developing a vision or image of what the organisation should be like in three or five years' time if it was operating on the basis of service quality.
- What is the current situation? An assessment of the extent to which the organisation curently accords with these values and the identification of major gaps or discrepancies.
- What steps are needed? A statement of the actions, decisions and changes which are necessary to move towards this vision. This should include an indication of time scale, responsibilities and resource implications.
- What are the supports and resistances? An analysis of those factors which will support the achievement of the strategy and those which may obstruct or hinder it. It could also include a consideration of how to increase positive forces and reduce those in opposition.

Attention should be paid to the process of developing the strategy, not least because the quality of relationships within the organisation have a significant effect on the quality of service to external customers (see Chapter 8). This poses several management issues. Firstly, *who is to be involved in developing the strategy?* It is rare for anyone other than managers and elected members to be included in working groups developing corporate or departmental policy on any topic, even though the effects will be felt by customers and employees. Service quality is an area where it is particularly important to have a broad base of membership in the strategy formulation process.

- Watford BC have established a customer service working group whose task is to develop a strategy and key tasks for the authority.

The group consists of employees across the organisation and at different levels in the formal hierarchy.

- Newcastle City Council shop stewards worked together with tenants' associations to review refuse collection and street cleansing services and produced a strategy for improving service quality in the context of CCT. The process included small workplace meetings to identify blockages and a survey of tenants groups' attitudes to the service. Some shop stewards were temporarily released from their normal duties to undertake this task.

Secondly, *what is their status?* Corporate working groups are often constituted on the basis of departmental representation. This may not be appropriate for a group developing a service quality strategy. Enthusiasm, interest, experience at introducing quality initiatives or representation by gender, ethnic origin, grade or type of job could be more appropriate criteria.

- Middlesbrough leisure services invited all employees, of whom there were approximately 140, to volunteer to join a group to review and develop proposals for improving the quality and equality of services. 50 per cent said they would like to take part and the final selection of 20 was made in terms of the criteria highlighted above.
- Derwentside established eight quality teams consisting of representatives from the DSO, front line and support services, different levels in the hierarchy and an elected member. Their role was to review existing activity in particular areas (listening to the public, internal communications, etc.) and produce recommendations for change. The teams had a six month life and generated 160 proposals for action.

Thirdly, *what is their task?* Is the group established purely to develop a strategy, its life ending once this has been adopted by the authority or is it to ensure that implementation also occurs? While time limited project groups have benefits in giving members a clear focus and not tying up organisational resources over a long period their disadvantage – as far as an issue like service quality is concerned – is that the expertise, knowledge and working relationships become dissipated and the momentum for change reduced. This consideration links closely to the fourth issue: *what is the implementation structure?* Implementation should be thought about at the same time as the strategy is being developed. This enables key relationships to be built, ideas to be tested out and a wider group of people to be involved in the shaping of the strategy.

Key components for a service quality strategy

The starting point should be understanding *who the organisation's customers are*. Ways of defining customers through their relationship to the local authority were discussed in Chapter 2 and elsewhere in the book other categorisations have been used – for example by age, geographical location, sex, car ownership, disability and ethnic origin. *Constraints to service quality* were also discussed in Chapter 2, and the issues raised there provide a checklist which an authority can use to assess its own situation. This will enable a mapping of *the current approach to service quality* using the grid in Figure 2.7.

From this basis *services can be reviewed* by employing the various techniques discussed in Chapter 3 and summarised in Figure 3.1. A key element here will be establishing the nature of *the relationship with customers* (and possibly also citizens) using the scale in Figure 3.2. This process of investigation will involve *analysis in terms of various criteria* including need, equality, fairness, economy and efficiency. These are considered in detail in Chapter 4.

At this point the strategy process should identify *the direction of change required* and its feasibility in the context of the particular local authority. Figure 2.7 can again be used to establish whether the authority is wanting to move towards customer care, community power or customer service. Clarifying the overall direction of change will enable better targeting of action and resources. Where the focus is towards customer care *redesigning the organisational arrangements and service relationship* will be particularly important. These are covered in Chapters 5 and 7. Attention should be given to *specifying the service package* (Chapter 5 and Figure 2.4) and *designing the customer process* (Figure 5.7). Figure 9.2 illustrates ways in which the constraints to service quality can be overcome. If the organisation wishes to enhance community power then it will need to focus on *citizenship and empowerment*. These are covered in Chapter 6. The authority should particularly identify ways in which *issues and demands are filtered out* before an explicit decision on them is made (see Figure 6.1).

Whatever the direction of change the *internal service relationships* will need to be redesigned. Chapter 8 covers the key issues of quality systems, front line/back line linkages and the manager's role. Particular attention should be devoted to *the culture* (Figure 8.2) and managers should be aware that they will only have a partial perspective on service quality. *Elected members* have a key part to play and ways of enabling them to develop their role should be identified (Chapter 6).

The two dimensions of service orientation and power which were used to map local authorities' approaches to external service quality can also be applied to an analysis of its *internal* management approach. Here the dimensions are managers' service orientation towards employees and the extent of employee power to take steps to improve any aspects of service quality. This gives four management approaches:

- Directive management – the traditional pattern of hierarchical manager–subordinate relations where employees have limited power and managers do not behave towards them in accordance with the principles of good service.
- Service management – characterised by managers being open and accessible to staff, encouraging quality of service to external customers and paying attention to hygiene factors in the workplace, but still retaining considerable power and limiting the opportunities for employees to develop their own solutions to quality problems.

Figure 9.2: Improving service quality

External Relationships

- *Information collection* – market research surveys; consultation exercises; ward meetings; user panels; 'phone-ins'; opinion cards at service outlets.
- *Information provision* – improved leaflets; translation and signing services; strengthened public relations; use of local media; open days; corporate image; public viewdata terminals; keeping employees and councillors informed.
- *Access* – improved reception facilities; single access points for range of services; neighbourhood offices; improved telephone systems; duty managers; managers on reception desks; physical access for prams and wheelchairs; complaints hot-lines.
- *Service delivery* – investing in employees through training, etc.; statements of customers' rights; service guarantees; develop problem-solving role of customer contact employees; redress and compensation systems; monitoring praise and complaints; removing job demarcation; investment in information technology; quality assurance systems.

Internal Operation

- *Performance indicators* – systematic public opinion polling; service sampling by managers; user involvement in service redesign; monitoring members' surgeries.
- *Organisational culture* – service days/teams; quality circles; devolving managerial responsibility and budgets; clarifying internal customer relationships; 'management by walking around'; quality-focussed recruitment, induction and training policies; 90 day challenge; internal secondments; 'patch'/neighbourhood focussed multi-disciplinary teams; total quality management.

- Individual initiative – a situation where employees have considerable discretion and autonomy in tackling quality problems but their effectiveness is limited because managers fail to develop a service relationship with them.
- Partnership management – this combines a redistribution of power to employees with significant service-oriented behaviour by managers.

Connecting the internal and external frameworks provides a way of reviewing and planning a parallel strategy for service quality (Figure 9.3). Any strategy should aim to ensure consistency between the two approaches. For example, continuing directive management internally while trying to move towards customer service externally is likely to provide a major contradiction for those employees expected to deliver high quality and responsive service to customers yet who find that their managers pay little attention to the quality of working relationships and are not responsive to their needs.

Figure 9.3: The management approach and the quality strategy

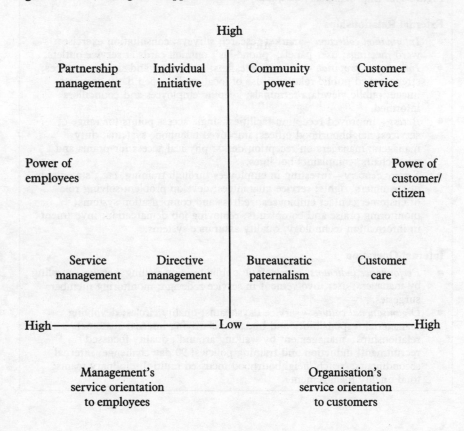

High

| Partnership management | Individual initiative | | Community power | Customer service |

Power of employees

Power of customer/ citizen

| Service management | Directive management | | Bureaucratic paternalism | Customer care |

High————————————Low ————————————High

Management's
service orientation
to employees

Organisation's
service orientation
to customers

Managing organisational change

Introducing service quality involves organisational change – people doing things differently, being aware of new issues, developing different forms of internal and external relationships, perhaps working in a restructured organisation. Two models for organisational change are the centralist and the seedcorn.

The centralist model involves the idea and its implications being worked out in detail at the top of the formal hierarchy and then imposed on the rest of the organisation using the resources at the centre's disposal – including power, money and patronage. It is a method of making those changes happen which the centre wishes to occur, but suffers from the drawback that those lower down the organisational hierarchy who have not previously been involved will have a low commitment to it. Additionally it is never possible for the centre to understand fully the situation elsewhere in the organisation and therefore the plan will never be completely appropriate.

The seedcorn strategy involves conveying the kernel of the idea throughout the organisation, encouraging employees to adopt it by providing support, encouragement and resources when requested and giving them the discretion to interpret it depending on their own situation. This can have a more profound effect on the organisation if the support is available, but it may take time to have any significant effect. Additionally anomilies between service areas can develop.

The fact that managers are seeking to introduce service quality should be the prime criteria in assessing which organisational change model to adopt. Taking the maxim 'managers should treat employees as they would like employees to treat customers' will lead to a bias in favour of the seedcorn approach. This will involve managers developing a facilitative style of leadership in which their role is to assist other employees to develop their own leadership potential and use their initiative in improving quality in their area of responsibility. Clarke and Stewart (1988, p.22) highlight aspects of this model of leadership in the context of the enabling council:

> It requires leadership which not only is capable of taking a strategic or corporate view but also encourages this at all levels in the organisation. It needs to demonstrate that it is not wedded to the concerns of a particular profession or service . . . Leadership itself needs to be enabling. This is to say, it needs to be helping and encouraging others both inside and outside the organisation to see issues, opportunities and needs and to respond. It is a leadership which is about empowering others to act.

Managers therefore have a central place in developing service quality. Their approach and behaviour can have a profound effect on the organisation and help or hinder moves to a greater customer and citizen orientation. Managing for service quality should be at the heart of the management task in local authorities.

References

Adam Smith Institute 1991 *Empowerment: The Theme for the 1990s.*

Association of District Councils 1991 *Customer Care: A Guide for Elected Members.*

Association of Metropolitan Authorities 1989 *Community Development: The local Authority Role.*

Association of Metropolitan Authorities 1990 *Contracts for Social Care: The Local Authority View.*

Association of Metropolitan Authorities 1991 *Quality Services: An Introduction to Quality Assurance for Local Authorities.*

Audit Commission 1983 *Code of Local Authority Audit Practice.*

Berry, L. 1988 'The rhetoric of consumerism and the exclusion of community' *Community Development Journal* 23(4).

Brooke, R. 1989 *Managing the Enabling Authority* Longman.

Chartered Institute of Public Finance and Accountancy 1991 *Service Level Agreements: A Compendium.*

Cheltenham BC 1990 *A Review of the Management Process.*

Clarke, M. and Stewart, J. 1988 *The Enabling Council* LGMB.

Clayton, S. 1983 'Social need revisited' *Journal of Social Policy* 12(2).

Corden, A. 1983 *Taking Up a Means-Tested Benefit: The Process of Claiming Family Income Supplement* DHSS HMSO.

Croft, S. and Beresford, P. 1989 'User-involvement, citizenship and social policy' *Critical Social Policy* 9(2).

Department of Education and Science 1991 *The Parent's Charter* HMSO.

Department of Social Security 1991 *The Right to Complain* Social Services Inspectorate HMSO.

Frater, M. 1990 'Implementing the vision through managerial responsibility' *Management Education and Development* 21(5).

Fry, G. 1987 'Outlining the next steps' *Public Administration* 65(2).

Fryer, P. 1984 *Staying Power: The History of Black People in Britain* Pluto Press.

Gould, M. and Campbell, A. 1987 *Strategies and Spoils: The Role of the Centre in Managing Diversified Companies* Blackwell.

Gutch, R. *et al.* 1990 *Partners or Agents? Local Government and the Voluntary Sector: Changing Relationships in the 1990s* National Council for Voluntary Organisations.

Hambleton, R. *et al.* 1989 'The decentralisation of public service: A research agenda' *Local Government Studies* 15(1).

Hancox, A. *et al.* 1989 'Developing a customer-oriented approach to service delivery: The Wrekin approach' *Local Government Studies* 15(1).

Hoggett, P. and Bramley, G. 1989 'The Devolution of Local Budgets' *Public Money and Management* 9(4).

James, K. 1989 'Encounter analysis: front-line conversations and their role in improving customer service' *Local Government Studies* 15(3).

Johnston, R. 1987 'A framework for developing a quality strategy in a customer processing operation' *International Journal of Quality and Reliability Management* 4(4).

Labour Party 1989 *Quality Street.*

Labour Party 1990 *A Better Deal.*

Labour Party 1991 *Citizen's Charter: Labour's Better Deal for Consumers and Citizens.*

LeGrand, J. 1983 *The Strategy of Equality* George Allen and Unwin.

Liberal Democrats 1991 *Shaping Tomorrow's Local Democracy* English Green Paper No. 5.

Local Authorities Conditions of Service Advisory Board 1990a *Performance Related Pay in Practice: Case Studies from Local Government.*

Local Authorities Conditions of Service Advisory Board 1990b *A Handbook on Performance Related Pay.*

Local Government Management Board 1987 *Getting Closer to the Public.*

Local Government Management Board 1989 *Learning From the Public.*

Local Government Management Board 1990 *A Local Authority's Options for Service Delivery.*

Local Government Management Board 1991 *Quality and Equality: Service to the Whole Community.*

Meade, K. and Carter, T. 1990 'Empowering older users: some starting points' in Winn, L. (ed.) *Power to the People: The Key to Responsive Services in Health and Social Care* Kings Fund Centre.

National Audit Office 1988 *Department of Health and Social Security: Quality of Service to the Public at Local Offices* HC451 HMSO.

Normann, R. 1984 *Service Management* Wiley.

Oakland, J. 1989 *Total Quality Management* Butterworth Heinemann.

Parasuraman, A. *et al.* 1985 'A conceptual model of service quality and its implications for future research' *Journal of Marketing* 49(3).

Peters, T. and Waterman, R. 1982 *In Search of Excellence* Harper and Row.

Potter, J. 1988 'Consumerism and the public sector' *Public Administration* 66(2).

Powell, M. 1990 'Need and provision in the NHS: an inverse care 'law'' *Policy and Politics* 18(1).

Prime Minister 1991 *The Citizen's Charter: Raising the Standard* Cm1599 HMSO.

Rogers, S. 1991 *Performance Review in Local Government* Longman.

Saunders, P. 1979 *Urban Politics: A Sociological Explanation* Hutchinson.

Seneviratne, M. and Cracknell, S. 1988 'Consumer complaints in the public sector' *Public Administration* 66(2).

Stewart, J. 1988 *Understanding the Management of Local Government* Longman.

Stewart, J. and Clarke, M. 1987 'The public service orientation: issues and dilemmas' *Public Administration* 65(2).

Stewart, J. and Walsh, K. 1989 *In Search of Quality* LGMB.

Stonefrost, M. 1990 *Encouraging Citizenship: Report of the Commission on Citizenship* HMSO.

Walsh, K. 1990 'Quality of service in housing management' in Harrop, K. and Fenwick, J. (eds) *Consumerism and the Public Services* Local Authority Management Unit Discussion Paper 90/1 Newcastle Upon Tyne Polytechnic.

Walsh, K. 1991 *Competitive Tendering for Local Authority Services: Initial Experiences* Department of the Environment HMSO.

Walsh, K. and Davis, H. 1991 *The Client Side in Competition* INLOGOV University of Birmingham.

Walsh, K. and Spencer, K. 1990 *The Quality of Management in the Housing Service* INLOGOV University of Birmingham.

Warwickshire CC 1990 *Management Delegation Project Report.*

Webster, B. 1990 'Reviewing services for the under-fives and their families in
    Gloucestershire' *Local Government Policy Making* 17(3)
Webster, B. 1991 *Customer Service in the Counties* Association of County Councils.
Widdicombe, D. 1986 *Report of the Committee of Inquiry into the Conduct of Local
    Authority Business* Research Volume 4 HMSO.
Winkler, F. 1987 'Consumerism in health care' *Policy and Politics* 15(1).
Yusuf, P. and Kettleborough, H. 1990 'Starting to give black women a voice in
    council services' *Community Development Journal* 25(2).

Index